NOTABLE WOMEN *of* ALABAMA

JOE CUHAJ

THE History PRESS

Published by The History Press
An imprint of Arcadia Publishing
Charleston, SC
www.historypress.com

First published 2025

Manufactured in the United States

ISBN 9781467159852

Library of Congress Control Number: 2025941509

This book is dedicated to the three most notable Alabama women in my life:
my wife, Maggie; my daughter, Kellie; and my granddaughter, Cora,
with much love.

CONTENTS

INTRODUCTION

History is a fascinating journey, a trip through time with many twists, turns and forks in the road. And if you dig deep enough, chances are that the journey will culminate in a surprise ending. Sometimes history is straightforward: stories of well-known personalities and major events that we all learned in our school days. But history can be much more than that; there are many little-known to unknown or forgotten figures who are rarely talked about but made their mark and changed the course of history in one way or another.

When I first moved to Alabama from New Jersey, over forty years ago now, I knew of the major players in the state's history: Martin Luther King Jr., George Wallace, Rosa Parks and so on. But as I wrote several other nonfiction history titles about little-known American and Alabama history, I discovered the stories of many remarkable Alabama women who played key roles in not only the state's history but the nation's history as well. I'd never been introduced to these women, and the more I read about them, the more I wanted to bring their stories to life.

This book traces the stories of fifty notable women of Alabama. Some of the names you will undoubtedly know. Some you might have heard of but never really heard their story. And others you may be introduced to for the first time, like I was. Some of the women within these pages were born in Alabama and then moved elsewhere to chart their course; others were born outside the state but moved here to make history; and still others were Alabama born and raised, choosing to remain in-state to use their talent and expertise to better life here in the State of Surprises.

The stories of these fifty women cover a wide variety of careers and experiences. You'll learn about women who led the way when it came to opening doors for women to participate in politics; the many women who fought as suffragists to earn women the right to vote; a number of women—both Black and white—who made a difference in the Civil Rights Movement; and of course, a number of incredible women who brought joy to the world through their music, from blues to pop to country and everything in between.

One thing you will notice as you turn the pages of this book is that a number of stories overlap, giving subjects we all know more depth and clarity. For example, we all know the story of Rosa Parks, who refused to give up her seat on a segregated Montgomery bus to a white woman, igniting the Montgomery Bus Boycott in 1955, but few people remember that another young woman, fifteen-year-old Claudette Colvin, was arrested and similarly charged only months before Parks's famous protest. And as the boycott began, one woman secretly fed the movement, helping to raise money and arrange transportation for those participating in the boycott: Georgia Gilmore. And that is only the beginning of how some of these stories intertwine with one another.

I have written several nonfiction history books over the years, and the first question I'm asked whenever I do a signing or presentation is: "How did you become so interested in documenting the history you write about?" Well, I consider myself very fortunate to have had some wonderful influences growing up in northern New Jersey, just outside of the Big Apple, who piqued my interest in history. The question I often ask myself is: Why didn't I pursue history as a career option? Being young and foolish, I had my heart set on becoming a radio announcer, which I did, and that's where life led me.

My biggest influences came from my family. Everyone in the Cuhaj household—my mom, dad, sister—all enjoyed learning about history. My mother and father could spout historical facts at a moment's notice. Both my sister and I excelled in history courses throughout our public school and college years. And that brings me to my second influence: my history teachers at good old Mahwah High School.

In my four years of high school, I had some of the best history teachers, who could make otherwise stodgy, dry, boring history come alive. They could take those sleep-inducing lists of dates out of the dustbin and bring them into the light to take us down the back alleys of history, where we would discover that there is much more to the subject than simply regurgitating facts and dates. Those teachers did all they could to avoid painting history with broad strokes. Instead, they would use a fine-tipped brush and enthrall us with amazing stories about the past, leaving us wanting more.

Those high school years also brought out the writer in me, offering fascinating courses in creative writing, journalism and the one that bolstered my desire to get into radio: a class called Mass Media, where we learned the ins and outs of radio, television and more.

When it came to history classes, one teacher stood out for me and really made an impression: Mr. Clough. I hope every student in public school has a Mr. Clough to inspire them. He could spit out historical facts and dates like nobody's business but with a comedic presentation. Never one for droning on about a subject, Mr. Clough always interjected humor into his teaching. To top it off, he had round wire-rim glasses and a big, burly moustache that made him resemble Groucho Marx. He even had the same delivery: every sentence was laden with a bad pun or a play on words. But the bottom line was: he got his lessons across to us. The wealth of knowledge he bestowed on us kids was phenomenal. He taught us the history behind the history.

To top it off, I must admit that I was a weird kid growing up in New Jersey. It was back in the 1960s, and living so close to New York City meant one thing for our household: newspapers. Lots and lots of newspapers. Some were delivered by a paperboy speeding down the road on his bike, hurling rolled-up editions at our house, taking out some of my mother's prized rose bushes or coming precariously close to smashing a window. Otherwise, I would pick up the Sunday papers each week. Every Sunday, my dad would send me on a mission to ride my bike downtown to a local newsstand and pick up the Sunday Jersey-centric *Bergen Record*, the *Daily News* and *The New York Times*. The Sunday edition of the *Times* was as thick as three Manhattan phone books stacked one on top of the other (you remember phone books, don't you?).

Our entire family would devour them all, reading every word from front to back. A couple of the papers had full-color comics on Sunday, and you would think that a boy of ten or eleven would automatically gravitate to those glorious color pages. Not me, and that's what made me a weird kid. I would sprawl out on the floor with a copy of the Sunday *New York Times* and head to the last section of the paper and the very last pages, like section G, page 46. Hidden deep within those pages, I would find obscure and offbeat news stories that fascinated me. They were no more than a short two or three paragraphs long and introduced me to the everyday lives of ordinary people from around the world. They were stories that never made the headlines and covered many different topics. Sometimes the stories were tragic, sometimes heartwarming, sometimes plain funny—and sometimes they left me shaking my head and wondering. They were stories that have long since been lost to time.

And that is how I became an armchair historian. The voices of Mr. Clough and my family ringing in my ears from all those years ago urged me on to write my (at press time) seven nonfiction history books, including three Mobile-centric titles for Arcadia Publishing and The History Press: *Baseball in Mobile*, *Hidden History of Mobile* and *A History Lover's Guide to Mobile and Baldwin County*. I remembered those days long ago, my teachers and my unique reading habits, and I wanted to use those memories to bring forgotten stories and biographies of Alabama personalities to life. I was getting back to my roots, as it were.

My goal in writing *Notable Women of Alabama* was not to present you with a stodgy, stuffy, date-riddled history book. Instead, my intent was to bring you the facts about the incredible Alabama women who shaped the state's history and that of the nation, including little-known tidbits of information you may not know or have forgotten. I hope you will be surprised, a little amused and maybe a little shocked when you read the stories of these remarkable women—but most importantly, I hope that this book is only the beginning of your own adventure to explore and learn more about many other fascinating Alabama women that I couldn't include. There are plenty more notable Alabama women who have a story to tell, hidden in the shadows, waiting to be discovered if we care to look for them.

Let's get started on our journey and meet fifty *Notable Women of Alabama*.

Chapter 1

MARYON PITTMAN ALLEN

The Southern Girl in the Senate

Maryon Pittman, born in Meridian, Mississippi, moved to Birmingham with her family as a youngster and knew what she wanted to do for a living: write. More specifically, she wanted to become a journalist.

Maryon went to college to study journalism at the University of Alabama, where she was known for being a strong, confident and independent hell-raiser, but she left academics behind when she married Joshua Mullins. The couple had three children before divorcing in 1958.[1]

Maryon found work in a Birmingham insurance office but found the job mundane. What she wanted to do was write society columns. She went to work as the women's section editor for several state weekly papers, including the *Shades Valley Sun*, and eventually moved up to writing for one of the largest newspapers in the state, the *Birmingham News*.[2] During her time at the *News*, Maryon met the state's lieutenant governor, James Allen, and the couple fell in love and married in 1964.[3]

James was on the fast track in the political world and was elected to the U.S. Senate in 1968. The couple moved to Washington, and Maryon continued her writing career, penning a syndicated column that appeared in Alabama newspapers called Reflections of a News Hen.[4] Meanwhile, her husband, a conservative Democrat, was making waves in the Senate, using his in-depth knowledge of Senate rules to slow or completely derail legislation that he disagreed with. His most notable challenge was to the bill that would turn the Panama Canal over to the country of Panama.

Senator James and Maryon Allen. *Library of Congress, Prints and Photographs Division.*

The couple was deeply in love, but tragedy struck on June 1, 1978. James stepped out of the bathtub in the couple's home and calmly said to his wife, "Honey, help me." The senator then quietly collapsed into her arms. James had suffered a heart attack, and as he lay in his wife's arms, he spoke his last words to her: "I love you, and don't forget that." James Allen died at the age of sixty-five.

With two years remaining in Allen's term, Governor George Wallace appointed Maryon to fill the vacant seat, making her only the second woman from Alabama to hold the position, the first being Dixie Bibb Graves in 1937. As an aside, to this date, only three women have held the seat. The third woman was elected in 2023: Katie Britt.

When asked for her reaction to the appointment, Maryon replied, "I have a penchant for being irreverent. I guess I'll have to be dignified now." That was Maryon's polite way of saying that the hardest thing she had to learn was to keep her mouth shut. And she wasn't good at that. During debates, she could be heard screaming at fellow senators, "You goddamn idiot!"

When he appointed Maryon, Governor Wallace made it quite clear that when her term was over, he would be running for the seat. In an interview with the *Washington Post*, Maryon spoke of her meeting with Wallace.[5]

Maryon told the *Post* that Wallace took a deep breath and said, "Of course, you know and understand, Maryon, that I'm going to be running, don't you?" There was a long silence. Wallace asked again, "Maryon, you do understand, don't you?" Again, Maryon was silent. Wallace finally said, exasperated, "Maryon, you're there, aren't you?"

This time, she answered, "Yes, George. I'm here."

Wallace asked, "Well? What do you say?"

Her final answer was to the point: "Nothing, George."

Women in the Pittman family had a motto: "Ain't nobody gon' run over a Pittman girl." And they didn't, not even George Wallace. In a 1998 interview with the Associated Press, Maryon said, "I want it chiseled on my tombstone that this 5-foot-2 woman who weighs 110 pounds kept George Corley Wallace out of the Senate."[6]

As the end of her appointment neared, Maryon Adams decided to toss her hat in the ring and make a run for the office, but her outspoken personality proved to be her campaign's undoing. In an interview for the *Washington Post,* a reporter told her that she was being interviewed for an article on the race along with several other Alabama women, including the sister of former Alabama governor "Big" Jim Folsom, the highly popular "Big Ruby" Folsom. "Honey," she told the reporter, "I got more couth than Big Ruby ever had. Even on my worst day."[7]

She went on to slam the Alabama governor himself.

> *To me, the worst thing a person can be is a bore. The cardinal sin. And they don't know they're bores. How can they not know? I think the Wallaces should shut up. It would be the Christian thing to do. Everybody in Alabama is getting tired of seeing those old dirty sheets flapping around on Perry Street* [the street where the governor's mansion is located].

In the end, Maryon was defeated in the Democratic primary by Donald Stewart. After the defeat, she swapped allegiances and supported the Republican candidate, James Martin. After leaving the Senate, Maryon remained in Washington and began writing a new weekly column, Maryon Allen's Washington. In her later years, she opened a highly successful vintage clothing restoration company. She passed away at the age of ninety-two.

---

1. Biographical Directory of the United States Congress, "Allen, Maryon Pittman," https://bioguide.congress.gov.
2. "Maryon Pittman Allen, 1925–2018," AL.com, July 19, 2018, https://obits.al.com.
3. Elbert L. Watson, *Alabama United States Senators* (Stroud, 1982), 150–52.
4. "Maryon Allen," Bhamwiki, https://www.bhamwiki.com.
5. Sally Quinn, "Maryon Allen: The Southern Girl in the Senate," *Washington Post,* July 30, 1978.
6. Associated Press, "Former U.S. Senator Maryon Allen Dies at 92," July 25, 2018.
7. William McDonald, "Maryon P. Allen, Made Senator by Death of Husband, Dies at 92," *New York Times,* July 27, 2018.

Chapter 2

EVELYN DANIEL ANDERSON

Inspiring Disability Advocate

It was a tragic accident that would change a young woman's life forever. On Christmas Eve 1930, in the town of Greensboro, Alabama, a child was playing with a .22-caliber gun. A stray bullet struck four-year-old Evelyn Daniel, causing irreparable damage to her spinal cord. Evelyn was paralyzed; she would never be able to walk or sit and would spend her life lying down, propped up by one arm. But despite her limitations, Evelyn grew to become a remarkable woman; her physical disability was not going to slow her down. Her disability, which she described as a "physical inconvenience," motivated her to pursue a career in teaching while at the same time becoming a staunch advocate for people with disabilities in the state. She graduated from Judson College, a private college for white women, with honors in 1948, earning dual degrees in art and history.

After graduating, Evelyn's first teaching job was as an art teacher at Greensboro High School; her title, however, was prefaced with the label "unofficial." That label was added because, at the time, Alabama law prohibited people with disabilities from teaching in public schools.[1] That was in 1948. By 1953, her dedication to the job and determination to make it work had caught the eye of a state legislator as well as the Alabama state school superintendent, who traveled to the statehouse to fight for the repeal of the discriminatory disability law and won.[2] Capable disabled persons were now officially able to teach in Alabama public schools.

Evelyn went on to earn a master's of education degree in counseling from the University of Alabama in 1964 and taught and counseled students in the Greensboro school system for thirty-four years before her retirement in 1982.[3] During that time, she was appointed to serve on the Alabama Governor's Committee on Employment of the Handicapped in 1977 and won numerous awards, including Outstanding Educator of the Year (1974), Alabama's Outstanding Counselor of the Year (1976) and the Alabama Handicapped Professional Woman of the Year Award (1977).

In an interview, Evelyn talked about whether she considered herself a role model. "Maybe I am an example. Without talking about myself, I hope I am. I've always been very proud and humbled to be a teacher. I think it is the most wonderful occupation there is. It's made me feel useful and, I guess, fulfilled."[4]

Evelyn passed away in 1998 at the age of seventy-two and was honored by being inducted into the Alabama Women's Hall of Fame in 2011.

---

1. Melissa Brown, "Rosa Parks, Condoleezza Rice, Coretta Scott King Among 10 Influential Women on Alabama List," *Montgomery Advertiser*, August 13, 2020.
2. Jeremy Gray, "An Alabama Teacher Overcame a Gunshot Wound, Paraplegia to Change State Law," AL.com, March 22, 2022, https://www.al.com.
3. "Evelyn Anderson (1926–1998)," Alabama Women's Hall of Fame, http://www.awhf.org.
4. Gray, "Alabama Teacher Overcame."

Chapter 3

MARY ANDERSON

An Inventor with "Vision"

It was an idea that would revolutionize the transportation industry—and one of those ideas where when you look at it, you think, *Wow. I should have thought of that.* It came in the early 1900s, a time when automobiles were just starting to make inroads (no pun intended) in replacing the horse and buggy as a mode of transportation—a time when horse-drawn streetcars were still the norm for mass transit. In 1902, Greene County native Mary Anderson was visiting New York City. It was a bitterly cold and snowy day as Mary hopped onto one of the city's many streetcars.

As the streetcar slowly moved through the narrow streets, the windshield became iced over with a thick layer of snow and sleet. The window was designed with two parts.[1] The bottom half of the window was stationary, while the top half, which was now covered in snow, could be opened so that the obstruction no longer blocked the driver's view. On this day, however, it was obvious that the design was not working. The inclement weather was so bad that the driver had to step out of the streetcar and clear the window by hand, and when he was able to open the window to see out, the icy cold northern wind whipped through the car, exposing the driver and his passengers to the inclement weather.[2]

Mary had an idea. Right there on the streetcar, she pulled out a pencil and a sheet of paper and began sketching a device that would revolutionize transportation.[3] Several designs later, she finally came up with a winner: a wooden arm with rubber attached to it. The arm would rest on the window

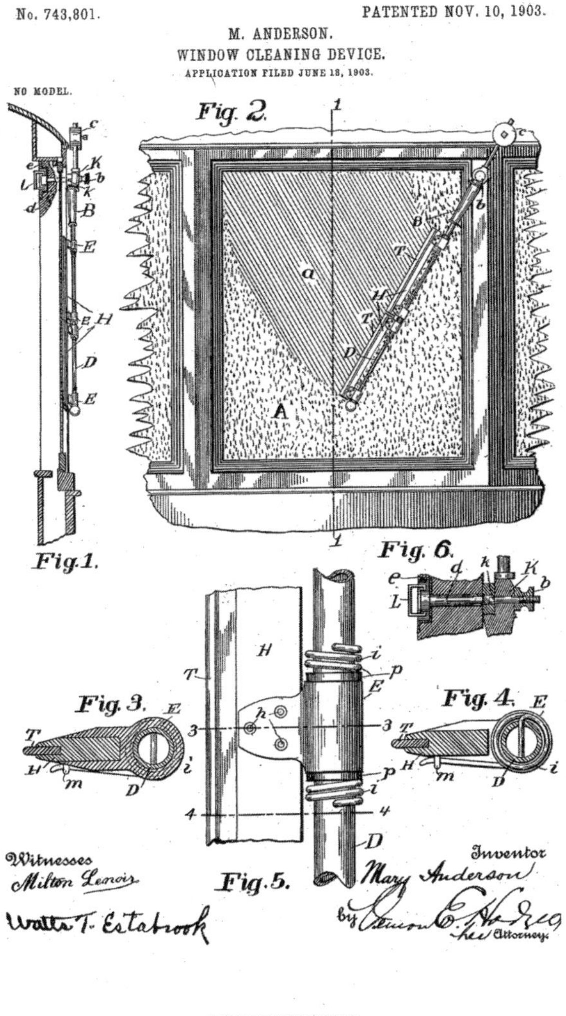

The 1903 design of Mary Anderson's window-cleaning device. *Public domain, via Wikimedia Commons.*

and be attached to a lever near the steering wheel. When the driver pulled the lever, the spring-loaded arm would sweep the snow, sleet and rain off the windshield and then return to its original position.[4] Mary Anderson had invented the windshield wiper.

Often, in the early twentieth century, when a new invention was announced, people scoffed at the idea. In Mary's case, the argument was that the device would distract the driver and cause accidents. Undaunted, Mary sent her sketches of the "Window Cleaning Device for Electric Cars and Other Vehicles to Remove Snow, Ice or Sleet from the Window" to the

U.S. Patent Office, and on November 10, 1903, she received a letter. Her invention had been patented and assigned patent number 743,801.

With a patent in hand, Mary sought to have the device manufactured but had little success. One reply, from the manufacturing firm Dinning and Eckenstein, read:

> *Dear Madam. We beg to acknowledge receipt of your recent favor with reference to the sale of your patent. In reply, we regret to state we do not consider it to be of such commercial value as would warrant our undertaking its sale.*[5]

In the end, Mary was unable to sell the patent on the device. In an interview with NPR, Mary's great-great-niece, the Reverend Sara-Scott Wingo, said the family believed the reason was that at the time, it was a male-dominated world, and being an independent woman may have done her in.[6] Whatever the reason, the patent expired, and Mary never capitalized on her invention, which would have an enormous impact on transportation around the world. In 1922, the first wipers were installed on Cadillacs, and they have been standard equipment ever since.

But rejection didn't stop Mary from becoming an entrepreneur in her own right, building and managing apartment buildings in Birmingham and a cattle ranch in Fresno, California. She passed away in 1953 and was inducted into the National Inventors Hall of Fame in 2011.

---

1. History.com Editors, "Mary Anderson Patents Windshield Wiper," History.com, November 13, 2009.
2. Kerry J. Byrne, "Meet the American Woman Who Invented Windshield Wipers, Mary Anderson, Alabama Entrepreneur," Fox News Media, May 31, 2024, https://www.foxnews.com.
3. Joe Palca, "Alabama Woman Stuck in NYC Traffic in 1902 Invented the Windshield Wiper," NPR, July 25, 2017, https://www.npr.org.
4. "Mary Anderson: Windshield Wiper," National Inventors Hall of Fame, https://www.invent.org.
5. Palca, "Alabama Woman Stuck."
6. Palca, "Alabama Woman Stuck."

Chapter 4

TALLULAH BANKHEAD

Living for the Moment

Traveling through Alabama, you might think that everything has the name Bankhead attached to it. There is the Bankhead National Forest, Bankhead Lake, Bankhead House and Heritage Center, Bankhead Highway and the Bankhead Tunnel in Mobile. There's a good reason for that. The Bankheads were once a powerful political family in the state. John H. Bankhead was a U.S. senator from 1907 to 1920. John H. Bankhead II was also a senator, from 1931 to 1946. Walter W. Bankhead was a congressman and a delegate to the Democratic National Convention in 1940. And the most famous of the Bankheads in politics was William Brockman Bankhead, who served in the U.S. House of Representatives, where he was elected House majority leader in 1935 and the forty-second Speaker of the House the following year.[1]

On January 31, 1902, in Huntsville, William B. Bankhead and his wife, Adelaide, became the proud parents of their second daughter, Tallulah Brockman Bankhead. Tallulah was named in part for her paternal grandmother and in part for a waterfall in Georgia, Tallulah Falls. It was a name that, she said, disgusted her. "Do you know what that name means?" she asked during an interview for her autobiography. "It disgusts me for people to think I made it up. I'd never think of a name like that. It means 'terrible.'"

Tallulah Bankhead would become a famous movie actress but is best known for her stage performances. She was also vocal in political matters, particularly select civil rights issues, but sadly, her complicated life is what most people remember. Biographer and historian Kari Frederickson said that while Tallulah was a "conventional liberal anti-communist, she was also brave enough to denounce those standing in the way of equality, her own family included."[2]

Tragically, Tallulah's mother passed away only weeks after giving birth to her, due to blood poisoning. The death left her father grieving, and he turned to alcohol, leaving his two daughters virtually alone. Their father sent them off to numerous boarding schools in Washington, D.C.—but not because he was searching for a better education for them. It was because Tallulah was a hard girl to tame and was prone to getting into trouble, which resulted in expulsions.

A portrait of actress Tallulah Bankhead. *Genthe photograph collection, Library of Congress, Prints and Photographs Division.*

With a flair for the dramatic, Tallulah decided to try her hand at acting, and at the age of fifteen, she submitted a photograph of herself to a movie fan magazine that proved to be the start of her career. She landed bit parts in several silent movies, starting in 1918. She made her first appearance on Broadway that same year, landing a role in the play *Squab Farm*. Her quick wit and what many described as her "dazzling stage presence," combined with her husky voice and stunning good looks, aligned to help Tallulah quickly climb the ladder to stardom.

The time she spent performing in London, England, proved that she was a star of the stage. Her performances were described as nothing less than spectacular during the 1920s, including her role in the Sidney Howard play *They Knew What They Wanted* in 1925.

Tallulah was never one for Hollywood, but in 1931, she signed a contract with Paramount Pictures, where she made six films that IMDb considers mediocre at best. She returned to New York and Broadway but did continue working in film, including the Academy Award–winning Alfred Hitchcock movie *Lifeboat*.

Bankhead grew interested in social movements in the 1930s, when she supported National Sharecroppers Week, an event that shined a spotlight on the hazardous working conditions of tenant farm workers in the South. In the 1950s, Tallulah used her name and fame to bring attention and funding to the Civil Rights Movement. She spoke out against lynchings and the disenfranchisement of Black Americans, pointing out that these were not only "Southern problems" but were also an issue in the North, where housing in urban areas was deplorable for people of color. She even spoke at civil rights rallies, including one held in New York City where she stood beside civil rights activist Rosa Parks and former First Lady Eleanor Roosevelt. In a 1960 interview with *Ebony* magazine, Bankhead said, "If you believe in something, say so loud enough to be heard."

But in the media, her complicated life was spotlighted more often than her activism. She led a hedonistic lifestyle. Tallulah was extremely promiscuous with both men and women. When appearing onstage, she would often dress in sheer lingerie, whether the role she was playing called for it or not. An excessive drinker and drug user, she was once quoted as saying, "My father warned me about men and booze, but he never mentioned a word about women and cocaine."

Tallulah continued acting on Broadway through the early part of the 1960s, but most of those performances were considered flops. Her last motion picture was the 1965 film *Die! Die! My Darling!*, in which she played a homicidal religious fanatic. She made one final appearance on television on May 14, 1968, when she appeared on *The Tonight Show with Johnny Carson* along with the Beatles John Lennon and Paul McCartney.[3] Seven months later, Tallulah Bankhead passed away at the age of sixty-six due to double pneumonia.

1. "Tallulah Brockman Bankhead (1903–1968)," Alabama Women's Hall of Fame, http://www.awhf.org.
2. Lyndsey Jenkins, "The Politics of Tallulah Bankhead—Ashley Steenson," Women's History Network, January 18, 2023, https://womenshistorynetwork.org.
3. Robert Gottlieb, "Dah-ling: The Strange Case of Tallulah Bankhead," *New Yorker*, May 8, 2005.

Chapter 5

REGINA BENJAMIN

America's Doctor

In 2020, the Centers for Disease Control and Prevention (CDC) released a study that found 15 percent of Americans live in rural areas. Residents living in these areas face an uphill battle when it comes to health care. Many live in what are deemed medical deserts, where there is a lack of hospitals, doctors or both. Residents in these regions tend to be underinsured (perhaps having no insurance at all) and are more likely to live in poverty. The report found that in 1999, people in rural communities had a 7 percent higher death rate than people living in urban areas. By 2019, that number had risen to 20 percent. One Alabama physician sought to change those numbers and, in the process, became the nation's top doctor, the eighteenth United States surgeon general: Dr. Regina M. Benjamin.

Dr. Benjamin was born in Mobile on the Alabama Gulf Coast on October 26, 1956, and was raised along Mobile Bay's Eastern Shore in the town of Daphne. Regina's parents divorced early on, and she was raised by her mother, who worked as a waitress and a maid to support the family. In an interview with Mobile's WKRG-TV, Regina recalled that growing up, she had never seen an African American doctor. In fact, she encountered very few African American professionals. Seeing that rural Alabama residents had few options when it came to health care, after graduating from Fairhope High School, she attended Xavier University in New Orleans, where she encountered her first African American medical doctors and went on to graduate with a degree in chemistry.

Surgeon General Regina Benjamin. *Office of the Surgeon General.*

Dr. Benjamin attended the Morehouse School of Medicine in Atlanta before transferring to the University of Alabama, where, at the age of twenty-eight, she earned her medical degree. Following her residency in family medicine, Dr. Benjamin returned to the Alabama Gulf Coast on a mission. After seeing her mother pass away due to lung cancer, her father die from hypertension and her brother pass away due to HIV, she took it on herself to open a new clinic in the tiny fishing village of Bayou La Batre, one of those rural medical deserts. Thanks to generous donations, grants and maxed-out credit cards, in 1990, the Bayou La Batre Health Clinic opened. The clinic was the only medical care facility for miles around, providing health care to anyone in need and charging patients only what they could afford—even paying for patients' prescriptions. The clinic also provided public educational programs on exercise and taught people about healthy eating and food preparation.

Dr. Benjamin presented one example of the clinic's mission during that interview with WKRG-TV. A homeless, disabled shrimper rode up to the clinic on his bicycle and asked for help after being struck by a car. Dr. Benjamin stopped what she was doing, tended to his injury, prescribed medications (paying for them herself) and then hugged the man and told him that he needed to stop smoking, which he promised to work on.

The clinic faced almost insurmountable obstacles when it was severely damaged in 1998 by Hurricane Georges and by Hurricane Katrina in 2005. Then there was a devastating fire in 2006. Dr. Benjamin clung to the dream and her passion and was able to keep the clinic open and rebuild it.

The opening of the clinic in 1990 was just the beginning for the young doctor, who now set her sights on a higher goal: to improve the nation's health care system. She authored numerous articles that received national attention, and she was presented with too many awards to mention here. Some notables include being named one of the Nation's 50 Future Leaders Aged 40 and Under by *TIME* and receiving the Nelson Mandela Award for Health and Human Rights and the 2000 National Caring Award, which was inspired by Mother Teresa.

All her hard work championing better health care nationwide, which included equal access to all no matter what their financial standing, reached a zenith in 2009 when President Barack Obama nominated her to be the eighteenth United States surgeon general. Her nomination was unanimously confirmed by the U.S. Senate. Soon after, Dr. Benjamin became the youngest person and the first African American admitted to the American Medical Association Board of Trustees. During her tenure as the nation's chief physician, she continued to be outspoken about the country's health care system—which caused a little bit of controversy when, in her first published paper in the position, she pointed out that low-income communities were more prone to obesity, specifically calling out women of color to exercise more.

Throughout her time as surgeon general and after she left the post in 2013, the clinic in Bayou La Batre remained open, providing needed health care to the community. At the same time, Dr. Benjamin was vocal in trying to prevent child sexual abuse and worked with the National Kidney Foundation to help find cures and treatments for kidney-related diseases, as well as suicide prevention. To this day, Dr. Regina Benjamin continues her work to provide better health care for all—she is, as *The New York Times* called her, a true "angel in white."

Chapter 6

YOLANDE BETBEZE

The Basque Spitfire

Some have called her America's Own Cinderella or Alabama's Cinderella, but there is only one nickname that truly suits Yolande Betbeze: the Basque Spitfire. Not only was Betbeze a former Miss America, but she also helped transform the pageant into more than just ninety minutes of beauty on parade, and from then on, she became an activist standing up for women's and civil rights, all the way up until her death in 2016.

Yolande Betbeze Fox, or Bebe as she was called by friends and family, was born in Mobile, Alabama, and raised in a strict Catholic home by her widowed mother. She attended school at Mobile's Visitation Convent. Yolande was quite happy to spend her days in the Mobile Public Library devouring books by Hegel, Sartre and Schopenhauer, but she also loved the opera and took six years of voice and ballet training. Yolande went on to attend Mobile's Springhill College, where, in 1949, she decided to enter the school's Miss Torch Contest and won the title.

After winning the Miss Torch Contest, Yolande had no intention of entering any other beauty pageants—that is, until a *Birmingham News* reporter heard her sing during a performance with the Mobile Opera Guild and convinced her to try out for the 1949 Miss Alabama pageant. Winning the state title would send her to Atlantic City to vie for the crown of Miss America and the chance of scholarships to continue her education.

With her hair in braids and still wearing braces on her teeth, Yolande performed songs by Schubert and made it through the preliminaries. After advancing to the finals, as Yolande put it, "It was off with the braces and

Miss America pageant contestant Yolande Betbeze. *New York World-Telegram and Sun Newspaper Photograph Collection (Library of Congress).*

on with the show." She won the title and headed to New Jersey. When Yolande arrived in the Garden State, pageant director Lenora Slaughter was quoted as saying she was "the sexiest, most glamorous thing I had laid my eyes on." And indeed she was. Her French Basque ancestry was evident in her mesmerizing dark brown eyes, lustrous dark hair and a smile that, biographers and reporters said, "ignited a room."

Yolande glided her way to the Miss America finals, where she was to sing an aria from Verdi's *Rigoletto* for the talent competition. During practice, she lost patience with the pageant's orchestra and requested that just the pianist accompany her. After only twenty minutes of rehearsal, Yolande hit the stage and brought down the house: the audience called her back for two encores. Two days later, she was crowned Miss America 1951. Reflecting on the moment years later, Yolande said, "There was nothing but trouble from the minute that crown touched my head." It wasn't bad trouble. It was just that the new Miss America had found her voice and was ready to use it.

It began the following morning, when Yolande had her first meeting with the press. It was obvious that this wasn't your typical Miss America. The men of the press began pelting her with the usual inane questions: Do you like to cook? What are your hobbies? When asked her opinion of men, she replied, "I haven't anything against men. I think they're here to stay."

The first big bombshell came soon after she was crowned. A major sponsor of the Miss America pageant, Catalina Swimwear, had signed an agreement with the pageant stating that whenever a contest winner made a public appearance, they would be required to wear one of the company's swimsuits. Whether intentionally or not, Yolande did not sign the agreement, and when it was time to make her first appearance, she flat-out refused to wear the outfit. "I'm a singer," she declared, "not a pinup!"

Catalina was incensed and threatened to pull its sponsorship. While it was a serious threat, pageant director Slaughter and the board of directors backed Yolande's decision. They released a statement saying that "we no longer permit our Miss America to go traipsing around the country in a bathing suit." Catalina did pull its sponsorship, but the pageant went on without it. Yolande's defiance of the requirement helped change the course of the beauty pageant, and her insurrection was rewarded when the fees charged for her appearances shot up, earning her over $50,000 that year.

But that wasn't the last we would hear of Yolande Betbeze. After her reign as Miss America, Yolande married Paramount movie executive Matthew Fox and gave birth to their daughter, Yolande Fox Campbell. She also became a social activist. In 1953, she participated in a vigil at Sing Sing Prison in New York to protest the upcoming execution of Julius and Ethel Rosenberg, who had been convicted of espionage. She picketed the Woolworth's in Times Square in support of Black sit-ins at the store's lunch counters across the country, telling the press, "I'm a Southern girl, but I'm a thinking girl."

She also joined protests against nuclear proliferation and volunteered with the NAACP and the Congress of Racial Equality (CORE) to demand racial equality regardless of race or gender. The latter caused Yolande to question the role of the Miss America pageant. At the time, the pageant permitted only white contestants. She publicly called on the pageant to change its ways and become all-inclusive. "It is a humiliation to every girl who enters the contest to feel that others just as pretty but of a different race are not free to compete with her." When asked to appear on the televised portion of one of the pageants in the 1960s, Yolande declined, saying, "Why would I want to do that? You're not Miss America. Y'all are Miss White Christian. When you include all ethnicities and religions, races, creeds, then you're Miss America, and then I'll be back." That change was slow to come, but it did, and in 1983, Vanessa Williams became the first Black Miss America.

Yolande continued her political activism for many years. Her husband, Matthew, passed away in 1964, and she and her daughter moved to Washington, D.C., where she purchased the house of former First Lady Jacqueline Kennedy. Yolande passed away while in hospice care in Washington in 2016 at the age of eighty-seven. Yolande was much more than a beauty queen. She will always be remembered as a feminist, a civil rights hero and a legendary Miss America.

Chapter 7

MARY LEE CAGLE

Pioneering Evangelist

Throughout history, women have fought an uphill battle. For centuries, men believed that a woman's place was in the home raising a family, and if women did join the workforce, they were relegated to menial tasks. Sadly, this form of discrimination still lingers to this day. It was much more evident in the 1800s, a time when it took an extraordinary woman to break through the status quo, smash perceived norms and carve a place out not only for herself but for future women as well.

In the late 1800s, a group of Southern women heeded their calling to preach the word of God and break through so called religious norms—the same belief that women needed to stay at home, raise families and not speak their mind publicly. This group of women found resistance every step along the way as they faced overwhelming prejudice and slander, all in an effort to spread God's Word. For example, in Batavia, Arkansas, Amanda Coulson felt the calling but was beaten down by malicious gossip and rumors that she had murdered her husband and abandoned her children, despite the fact that her husband, the Reverend D.M. Coulson, was alive and the couple did not have children.

One of those women who beat the odds was Mary Lee Cagle, who formed one of the largest congregations in the South. Born in Lawrence County near the town of Moulton in 1864, Mary was the daughter of farmers John and Nancy Wasson. The family were Methodists, and by the age of fifteen, Mary felt in her heart that she was being called to become a preacher. Of course, at the time, that was a radical notion, and her family pushed back on the idea in an attempt to squelch her ambitions.

It was in 1891 that Mary married Texas revivalist and Methodist Episcopal preacher Robert Lee Harris. For the next three years, Mary learned about evangelism from her husband as they crisscrossed the South through Kentucky, Tennessee, Mississippi and Alabama, holding revivals. In 1894, the couple landed in Milan, Tennessee, where, breaking with the Methodist Church, they founded the New Testament Church of Christ. The church quickly drew devout followers, but its success was short-lived, as Robert died of tuberculosis only months after the church was founded.

Along with two other women from the congregation, Donie Mitchum and Elliot Sheeks, Mary took the bold step of establishing new churches in Tennessee and Arkansas. In 1895, Mary established a congregation in Abilene, Texas, where she became pastor, evangelist and superintendent. Convincing churchgoers that women could be pastors was still an uphill battle, but the women's efforts would soon pay off.

After Mitchum and Sheeks became ordained ministers in 1901, Mitchum asked if she could preach a service at a church in Bells, Tennessee, which was met with fierce opposition from the congregation. Mitchum, however, was allowed to proceed with her sermon, which dealt with the question of whether women should preach the Gospel or not. As Mitchum later wrote:

> *July 21st, 1901, Sunday. Some of the opposers to women preaching were objecting to me holding the service at Cade's* [chapel] *last Sunday, quoting the text, "Let the women keep silence in the churches etc." trying to prove that Paul meant women* [are] *forbidden to preach or hold public services.... The Holy Ghost was poured out on us as I talked & gave them God's word for my arguments. The congregation seemed to melt down & at the close of my discourse quite a number shook my hand (who once opposed the doctrine of women preaching) with tears in their eyes & said "I endorsed your sermon Sr. Mitchum, go on & preach & do all the good you can."*

Under the leadership of Mary Lee Cagle, the three women continued their work and created what would become the Church of the Nazarene, one of the largest Christian denominations in the world. Today, the Church of the Nazarene proudly boasts of having 30,747 churches in 167 countries with over 2.7 million members, all thanks to the drive and ambition of Mary Lee Cagle.

Chapter 8

CLAUDETTE COLVIN

A Young Profile in Courage

Rosa Parks is an icon of the Civil Rights Movement. Her courage in refusing to give up her seat on a Montgomery city bus to a white passenger and move to the Black section was a defining moment in the movement that ignited a boycott by Black residents of Montgomery's mass transit system. Ten months before Rosa Parks made history, however, another woman, fifteen-year-old Claudette Colvin, summoned the courage to challenge the racial segregation laws of the Montgomery City Code the same way Rosa Parks would do a few months later.

In the 1940s and 1950s South, Jim Crow laws were established not only to separate the races but also to keep Blacks poor—or, as some described it, keeping Blacks under control from "womb to tomb."[1] At the age of four, Claudette had her first encounter with the Jim Crow South:

> *I was standing in line at the general store when this little white boy cut in front of me. Then some older white kids came in through the door and started laughing... They were pointing at me. The little white boy said, "Let me see, let me see, too." For some reason they all wanted to see my hands. I held my hands up, palms out, and he put his hands up against mine. My mother saw us and saw that the boy's mother was watching. Then my mom came straight across the room, raised her hand, and gave me a backslap across the face. I burst into tears. She said, "Don't you know you're not supposed to touch them?" The white boy's mom nodded at my mom and said, "That's right, Mary."*[2]

Eleven years later, on March 2, 1955, Claudette's school was let out early after a half day of classes. She climbed aboard the city bus that would take her home and presented the driver with a ticket that allowed students to ride for half price. When she stepped on board, there were no white passengers on the bus, so she took a seat in what was considered the white section. As the bus rumbled on, more and more white passengers boarded, until eventually there were no more seats in the white section, leaving one woman standing in the aisle, hovering over Claudette. Several times, the driver demanded that the girl give up her seat—but, as Claudette recalled, she was feeling rebellious. She had been studying the Constitution in school, and through her involvement with the local NAACP youth council, she knew her Fourteenth Amendment rights.[3]

When the bus arrived at a transfer point, a transit policeman climbed on board. At about the same time, Claudette's neighbor Mrs. Hamilton sat down next to her. The policeman ordered the two women to stand up and move to the back of the bus. Mrs. Hamilton, who was pregnant, said she didn't feel like it. Neither did Claudette.

The transit officer did not have the authority to arrest Claudette, but a block down the road, a police squad car was waiting. Claudette began crying and shouting, "It's my constitutional right to sit here as much as that lady!"[4] Colvin and three classmates—Aurelia S. Browder, Susie McDonald and Mary Louise Smith—were arrested. A short article appeared in the March 19, 1955, edition of *The New York Times* with the headline "Negro Girl Convicted."[5] The girls were charged with violation of the city's bus segregation policy. Claudette's minister paid her bail. During the trial, she pled not guilty; the judge decided otherwise and gave her probation.[6]

The girls were named plaintiffs in a lawsuit against the city, *Browder vs. Gayle*, in which the U.S. District Court of Alabama ruled that the segregation policy violated the Fourteenth Amendment. The case went to the U.S. Supreme Court, which upheld the lower court ruling.

Ten months after Claudette Colvin challenged Montgomery's segregation laws, another civil rights icon, Rosa Parks, refused to give up her seat on a city bus, and soon after, the Montgomery Bus Boycott began, but the protest actually began with a brave fifteen-year-old schoolgirl, Claudette Colvin.

---

1. Phillip Hoose, *Claudette Colvin: Twice Toward Justice* (R.R. Donnelley & Sons, 2009), 3–4.
2. Hoose, *Twice Toward Justice*, 3.

3. Tina Ligon, "60th Anniversary of the Montgomery Bus Boycott," *National Archives Rediscovering Black History* (blog), December 1, 2015, https://rediscovering-black-history.blogs.archives.gov.
4. Hoose, *Twice Toward Justice*, 34.
5. *New York Times*, "Negro Girl Convicted," March 19, 1965.
6. "Claudette Colvin," Biography.com, February 8, 2024, https://www.biography.com.

Chapter 9

LAVERNE COX

Born as Who We Are

Being a teenager is tough enough as you try to navigate your way through a myriad of life's obstacles. But imagine that as a preteen, you were also trying to find your identity and realizing that there was another side to you and it was something you had to deal with virtually on your own: the realization that you had inclinations that went against your assigned sex at birth. Instead of being male, you were more feminine. And that's where the story of Laverne Cox, actress and tireless advocate for LGBTQ+ rights, begins.

Laverne and her twin brother were born on May 29, 1972, in Mobile, Alabama, and raised by a single mother. Laverne was very creative and, at a very early age, dreamt of performing onstage. As early as fourth grade, she was taking tap and jazz dancing lessons but not ballet—her mother deemed that too feminine for a boy.

By the time she turned ten, she was feeling embarrassed by her feminine inclinations, brought on by what she called "major" bullying and harassment from not only schoolmates but adults as well for not "acting the way someone assigned male at birth is supposed to act."[1] Add to that the pressure of the teachings at her church and the passing of her grandmother, whom she believed was looking down at her disapprovingly. The emotions were too much, and she attempted suicide at age eleven.[2]

After the episode, Laverne turned her life around and received a scholarship to study at the Alabama School of Fine Arts in Birmingham. From there, she earned a scholarship to attend Indiana University and then

Laverne Cox. *Daga Luke Harold.*

transferred to Marymount Manhattan College in New York City. There, Laverne earned her BA in fine arts in dance. That's also where she decided that she wanted to become an actress. More importantly, during her time at Marymount, Laverne began the process of medical transition and began living and identifying as female.

Laverne made numerous appearances in off-Broadway productions, but what really changed her career path was seeing the 2007 television soap opera *Dirty Sexy Money*, starring Candis Cayne.[3] Cayne was the first openly transgender actor to have a recurring role on primetime television. And with that, Laverne knew that there was a chance of breaking into the medium.

After appearing on two episodes of NBC's *Law and Order*, Laverne landed a career-making role as Sophia Burset in the wildly successful 2012 Netflix show *Orange Is the New Black*, a role recognized by *TIME*, which called Burset the "most dynamic transgender character in history." Laverne is also the first openly transgender person to appear on the covers of *TIME*, *British Vogue* and *Essence*, among others. Laverne has used her success to be an outspoken advocate for the transgender community and LGBTQ+ rights in general, touring the country to make the case for equal rights with her presentation, *Ain't I a Woman?*[4]

---

1. "Person: Laverne Cox," Robert F. Kennedy Human Rights, December 6, 2023, https://rfkhumanrights.org.
2. Katy Steinmetz, "Laverne Cox Talks to *TIME* About the Transgender Movement," *TIME*, May 29, 2014.
3. "Laverne's Story," LaverneCox.com, January 17, 2017, https://lavernecox.com/about/.
4. Steinmetz, "Laverne Cox Talks to *TIME*."

Chapter 10

MARTHA FOSTER CRAWFORD

Alabama's First Foreign Missionary

Martha Foster Crawford was an inquisitive child with many interests but was especially interested in the welfare of women, both their physical and mental health as well as their spiritual welfare.[1] After a severe illness, Martha would feel a spiritual calling and, through a unique set of circumstances, be drawn into foreign missionary work, becoming the first foreign missionary from Alabama. As Baptist minister Joseph Borum wrote in 1880, Foster's service to God would "be remembered as long as the sun and moon endured."[2]

Born to Pastor John and Susanna Foster on January 28, 1830, in Jasper County, Georgia, Martha was the couple's fourth child. In October 1845, the family relocated to Tuscaloosa County, Alabama, where her father presided over the Grant's Creek Church. Four years later, Martha suffered from typhoid fever, a near-death experience that brought the young woman closer to God. She felt a spiritual calling to do missionary work abroad, particularly in China. With the backing of the Reverend E.B. Teague, Martha was recommended for a position doing missionary work by the Foreign Mission Board of the Southern Baptist Convention. Although she came highly recommended for the position, the board would not consider a single woman for the job.

In 1850, her letter of recommendation was shown to Tarleton Perry (T.P.) Crawford, a missionary evangelist from Kentucky. Seeing that this could be a beneficial relationship for both of them, he set out for Alabama, where he met Martha. The couple married three weeks after meeting.[3] The bride and groom spent their honeymoon at the 1851 Southern Baptist Convention, where Martha spoke before the assembly. The Alabama delegation was enthralled with her speech and believed her to be a visionary woman.[4] And with that, the missionary board made her its first foreign missionary and first female missionary from Alabama, dispatching her and T.P. to Shanghai on January 6, 1851.

The assignment was daunting and frightening, to say the least. Wars were being waged across the provinces, and the Chinese were very wary of foreigners. "Were it not for the fear and consequences restraining this government and people," she once wrote, "our heads would not remain for a day on our shoulders. The bitter opposition to foreigners, from the European to the beggar, is ineradicable, and restrained only by fear."[5] Her mission to bring the word of God to millions of people in China at times seemed overwhelming, as she wrote in an 1880 edition of the Baptist publication *The Watchman*:

> *This momentous responsibility of being trustees to receive and dispense the news of Christ's salvation to those who had never heard them, who are dying at the rate of 50,000 per day, often staggers me and leads me to careful examination of myself, how I stand before God and these lost millions. Spurgeon says, in reply to the man who had asked him if the heathen would be saved without the gospel, "The question is whether you will be saved if you do not send it to them."*[6]

Despite the danger and the overwhelming work with which she was charged, Martha Foster Crawford's missionary work continued across China from 1852 until her death in 1909.

---

1. "Martha Foster Crawford (1830–1909)," Alabama Women's Hall of Fame, http://www.awhf.org.
2. Joseph H. Borum, "Tarleton Perry Crawford, Martha Foster Crawford," Baptist History Homepage, http://baptisthistoryhomepage.com.
3. Borum, "Tarleton Perry Crawford."
4. "Martha Foster Crawford," Alabama Women's Hall of Fame.
5. Borum, "Tarleton Perry Crawford."
6. Martha Foster Crawford, "Our Duty to the Lost," *Watchman*, February 2, 1888, https://dukelibraries.contentdm.oclc.org/digital/collection/travdiaries/id/30171.

Chapter 11

NANCY BATSON CREWS

Alabama's First Lady of Flight

Ten months after the United States declared war on Japan and joined the fight in Europe during World War II, production of ships, armaments and aircraft increased exponentially. We know the story of the women who did their patriotic part for the war effort by taking to factories across the country to build the hundreds of planes and ships that would be needed to win the war—the "Rosie the Riveters." But women contributed in other ways to help win the war. One of the most important tasks they undertook, albeit limited to an exclusive group of women, was shuttling aircraft from factories to airfields across the country as part of the Women's Auxiliary Ferrying Squadron, or WAFS.

The WAFS were formed in September 1942 with one mission: to ferry U.S. Army Air Force (USAAF) light planes and trainers from factories to destinations across the country. The service would eventually ferry bombers, fighters and transport planes as well. The WAFS would be composed of no more than twenty-eight women, all of whom were required to have five hundred hours of flying time and a list of additional ratings.[1] And that's where the story of our next notable Alabama woman begins: Nancy Batson Crews, one of the WAFS "Originals."

Born in Birmingham on February 1, 1920, Nancy was the third of Stephen and Ruth Batson's four children. Her parents were strong-willed, athletic and disciplined, and they raised their children to be the same.[2] Nancy's parents described her as the "different" child: instead of a ballerina dress for her birthday or Christmas, she asked for an aviator scarf and jodhpurs, those wide-winged aviator trousers. Her parents were happy to oblige.[3]

Nancy E. Batson, WAFS pilot. *U.S. Air Force Photo.*

Following high school, Nancy attended college at the University of Alabama, where she received a private pilot certificate in the Civilian Pilot Training Program. In 1941, her parents bought her a plane—a Pope J-4 Cub Coupe, which she used to obtain her commercial pilot's certificate with instructor rating. Eventually, she was hired by Pan American Airways as a control tower trainee.[4]

By October 1942, Nancy had enough flying time and ratings to be accepted by the newly formed WAFS. Her first ferrying job came one month later, when she shuttled a PT-19 trainer from Hagerstown, Maryland, to a U.S. Army training base in Chattanooga, Tennessee. Eventually, she was tasked with shuttling fighter planes, including the P-47 Thunderbolt, becoming the first woman to do so.

One of the harrowing tales Nancy told during an interview with biographer Sarah Byrn Rickman for the book *Nancy Baston: Alabama's First Lady of Flight* occurred during a flight on election day 1944, when President Roosevelt won his unprecedented fourth term in office.[5] Nancy was to fly a brand-new, hot-off-the-assembly-line P-38 Lightning from the Lockheed plant in Long Beach, California, to Newark, New Jersey. The aircraft was known to have a few engine problems, one of which claimed the life of another member of the WAFS, Evelyn Sharp.

After making a stop in Pittsburgh to refuel, Nancy began the final leg of her journey to New Jersey. Soon after takeoff, she noticed the cooling gauges were acting strangely. Instead of flying on to New Jersey, she radioed the control tower in Pittsburgh and requested permission to return to the airfield. On her approach, she lowered the landing gear—and learned the true meaning of the words "flying by the seat of your pants." Nancy didn't feel the landing gear lower and lock in place. Then the control panel lit up, indicating that the nose wheel had not lowered. Checking special aluminum reflectors attached to the aircraft, she could see that the indicator was correct.

After doing a flyby of the tower so that controllers could confirm there was an issue, Nancy tried using a special hydraulic pump that would lower the nose wheel in the event of an emergency, but it didn't work. She pulled back on the wheel, climbed to an altitude of eight thousand feet and then put the aircraft into a steep dive, hoping that the force would dislodge the wheel. That didn't work, either.

In the control tower, the controller made a phone call to the WAFS operation officer, Nancy Love, to update her on the situation. "Who is it [in the plane]?" Love asked. The controller replied that it was Nancy Baston. "Oh, don't worry about her," Love replied. "She'll be fine."

Nancy knew that there was a special CO_2 cartridge in the plane that could be used in a last-ditch effort to lower the nose wheel. The engineers at Lockheed had told her emphatically not to use it because the landing gear could be severely damaged. But what choice did she have? Nancy reached under her seat and fired the cartridge. There was a blinding cloud of smoke, and when it cleared, the instrument panel showed that all the landing gear was down and locked. She verified this by checking the reflector mirrors and landed the plane safely. The plane rolled to a stop, where she was greeted by the ground crew. As she climbed out of the cockpit, she calmly said, "Boys, you have a real lemon here."

By the time the WAFS were ordered to stand down on December 20, 1944, Nancy Baston had accumulated over nine hundred hours in the air and flown twenty-five different types of aircraft, including the famous P-51 Mustang.[6] In 1946, she married Lieutenant Colonel Paul Crews, with whom she had three children. She continued training pilots at Rose Aviation in California, raced in three Powder Puff Derbies and later was elected as mayor of California City, California. Nancy Baston Crews was inducted into the Alabama Aviation Hall of Fame in 1989.

---

1. "Women's Auxiliary Ferrying Squadron," National Museum of the United States Air Force, https://www.nationalmuseum.af.mil.
2. Deborah G. Douglas, "Nancy Baston Crews: Alabama's First Lady of Flight," *Alabama Review* 63, no. 4 (October 2010), 298–99.
3. Sarah Byrn Rickman, *Nancy Baston Crews: Alabama's First Lady of Flight* (University of Alabama Press, 2009), 12.
4. "Nancy Baston Crews," CAF Rise Above, April 3, 2020, https://cafriseabove.org.
5. Rickman, *Nancy Baston Crews*, 6–10.
6. "Nancy Baston Crews," CAF Rise Above.

Chapter 12

ANGELA DAVIS

Philosopher, Activist, Political Prisoner

Angela Davis became one of the most famous political activists of the 1960s, and to this day, she continues her role as a prominent activist for a variety of issues, from civil rights to LGBTQ+ rights to women's rights.

Angela was born in Birmingham in 1944, the oldest of four children born to Frank and Sally Davis. When she was four, the middle-class family moved into a white neighborhood in the city, one several other Black families had settled into. A few months afterward, several of the homes were bombed by the Ku Klux Klan, and the neighborhood became known as Dynamite Hill.[1] Angela's mother would not stand idly by while the Klan terrorized their neighbors and became a vocal activist herself, joining the Southern Negro Youth Conference, whose leaders and organizers had communist leanings.[2]

Angela's parents made sure she had a well-rounded education, and she excelled in school. She was also a member of the Girl Scouts and attended Sunday school regularly. Angela spent her junior year of high school in Greenwich Village, New York, thanks to a program that was designed to help integrate northern schools and give white northern students exposure to the southern Black experience. The values and progressive attitudes instilled in Angela by her parents were reinforced by her experience in the Village, and she joined the school's communist youth group.[3]

After graduation, she attended Brandeis University in Massachusetts, where she earned a scholarship to study French in Paris. While in Europe, she earned a PhD in philosophy and participated in rallies with the Socialist German Student Union. During her time in Europe, a tragic event occurred in her hometown: the Sixteenth Street Baptist Church bombing that killed four young girls: Denise McNair (eleven), Addie Mae Collins (fourteen), Carole Robinson (fourteen) and Cynthia Wesley (fourteen), all of whom were friends of the Davis family.[4] The event threw Angela into grief and anger.

After returning to the United States in 1968, she joined the Black Panther Party, the Student Nonviolent Coordinating Committee and the Che-Lumumba Club of the Communist Party. When she finally completed her degree, Angela accepted a position as professor of philosophy at the University of California, Los Angeles (UCLA). It wasn't long after she accepted the position that the campus newspaper, *The Daily Bruin*, published an article that exposed Angela as a communist. The article, as it later turned out, was written not by a student at the college but by an undercover FBI agent.

Angela was questioned by school administrators. During the interviews, she admitted that she did indeed belong to groups that had communist leanings. Despite a California law stating that communist beliefs did not make an individual ineligible for employment, Governor Ronald Reagan pushed the issue, and Davis was removed from her position. She fought her removal, and with the backing of fellow professors and a decision by the California Supreme Court, UCLA was forced to reinstate her, but the incident had brought national attention to Angela. With her large, full Afro, she became the image of a militant Black woman. But the publicity was rarely good, and Angela found herself the recipient of many death threats, prompting her to move several times, hire security and purchase guns for her protection.

When her contract at UCLA expired in 1970, Davis went on to become an activist for prison reform and campaigned for the release of the Soledad Brothers, three prisoners who were falsely accused of murdering a prison guard at California's Soledad Prison. In a press conference, Davis said that the charges were the latest in a "long series of repressive and genocidal measures taken by the prisons in the state."[5]

On August 7, 1970, at the Marin County Courthouse, where the brothers were standing trial, Jonathan Jackson, the brother of one of the Soledad prisoners and a friend of Angela's, burst into the courthouse with a bowling bag full of weapons and took the judge and four others hostage. The hostage situation ended with a barrage of gunfire and the death of the judge. It was later discovered that the guns used in the incident had been purchased by Davis.[6]

Initially, the Marin County attorney general stated that Davis was not responsible in any way for the crime. Under incredible public and political pressure, the attorney general relented: a warrant was issued for Angela's arrest, and she was charged with being an accomplice to the crime. Angela had nothing to do with the courthouse kidnapping, but FBI Director J. Edgar Hoover and the public thought otherwise, and soon, Hoover placed Angela Davis on the FBI's Ten Most Wanted Fugitives list. In her autobiography, Davis writes about stealing away from her home under the cover of darkness to escape and the fear that overwhelmed her:

> *Outside in the open, entangled in my grief and anger was also fear. A plain and simple fear so overwhelming that the only thing I could compare it to was the sense of engulfment I used to feel as a child when I was left alone in the dark....I could feel a presence that I could describe easily. Images of attack kept flashing in my mind...clear pictures of machine guns breaking out of the darkness, surrounding Helen* [her friend] *and me, unleashing fire.*[7]

On October 13, FBI agents tracked down Angela and arrested her at a Howard Johnson's Motor Lodge in New York City. She surrendered peacefully and was jailed after being denied bond. The response by people around the world was swift, and the "Free Angela Davis" movement began. Thousands of people marched in protest against what they believed was a "political frame-up" and Angela being held as a political prisoner. Buttons and posters were seen everywhere. Over $500,000 was raised for her defense. Two of the most vocal and famous activists of the day, former Beatle John Lennon and his wife, Yoko Ono, even released a song, "Angela," on their *Sometime in New York City* album that spotlighted her plight and brought more attention to the injustice.

As the case against Angela was drawing enormous attention in the city, a change of venue motion was granted, and her trial took place in Santa Clara County, California. After thirteen hours of deliberation, on June 4, 1972, an all-white jury returned not guilty verdicts, and the case and charges were dismissed.

During her time in jail, Angela began working on prisoner's rights advocacy. "As soon as the trial was over," she told the PBS news show *Frontline*, "we tried to use the energy that had developed around my case to create [an] organization, which we called the National Alliance against

Racist and Political Repression….I'm still working for the freedom of political prisoners."

To this day, Angela advocates for the rights of political prisoners. She has written numerous works on racial politics and injustice, advocated for Palestinian rights and been a part of the Occupy movement. She was also named the honorary co-chair of the Women's March on Washington that opposed the election of Donald Trump as president in 2016. Angela continued teaching until her retirement in 2008.

1. Nelson George, "Angela Davis," *New York Times*, October 19, 2020.
2. "Angela Davis," Encyclopedia of Alabama, January 9, 2008, https://encyclopediaofalabama.org.
3. "Life Story: Angela Davis (1944–)," New York Historical Society, November 19, 2020, https://wams.nyhistory.org.
4. "Four Black Girls Killed in Church Bombing in Birmingham, Alabama," Equal Justice Initiative, https://calendar.eji.org.
5. Antonio Mejias-Rentas, "How Angela Davis Ended Up on the F.B.I. Most Wanted List," History.com, January 25, 2023.
6. "The Making of a Radical," *New York Times*, August 23, 1970.
7. Angela Y. Davis, *Angela Davis: An Autobiography* (International Publishers, 1996), 4–5.

Chapter 13

MAHALA ASHLEY DICKERSON

Delayed Justice for Sale

Determination: it's what drives people to overcome the odds and make the world a better place. Such is the story of Mahala Ashley Dickerson, who for well over sixty years fought against discrimination in the courtroom for countless people not only in Alabama but in Indiana and, eventually, Alaska as well.

Mahala was born in Montgomery in 1912. She credits her drive and ambition to make the world a better place and seek justice for the repressed to her school days at Miss White's Industrial School for Girls. The school was established by two white women from the Northeast, Alice White and H. Margaret Beard, in 1886. Their mission was to provide a rigorous Christian education, vocational training and academics for young Black girls from kindergarten to eighth grade.[1] Both Mahala and civil rights activist Rosa Parks, her classmate, credit their teacher Alice White with imparting to them the sense that they were equals with any race. "She would take two roses," Dickerson told WSAZ-TV reporter Maria Downey in 2004, "a white one and a pink one, and say, 'You are all a part of God's flower garden. Do you think God loves this white rose any more than he loves this pink rose?'"[2]

Following high school, Dickerson attended college at Fisk University in Tennessee in 1935 and then graduated with a law degree from one of the most prestigious Black universities in the United States, Howard University School of Law in Washington, D.C. Returning to Alabama in 1948, Mahala became the first Black female attorney in the state and began to work on discrimination and civil rights cases. She recalled that her most notable trial was of a woman and her six children who were being held in peonage, a form of slavery where laborers are bound in servitude because of debt—in their case, on a plantation. The mother had left the plantation without a required pass. In retaliation, the landowner held the children while the sheriff arrested the woman but did nothing to the landowner. Mahala took up the case and won. The family was reunited, but Mahala never believed that she did anything special: "I didn't think I did anything, really. I just happened to be there, the situation arose, and I did what anybody would have done."[3]

For the next sixty years, Mahala Dickerson fought for those facing discrimination—but not only in Alabama. In 1951, she relocated to Indiana, where she became only the second Black woman admitted to the Indiana Bar Association. She spent seven years practicing law in the Hoosier State. In 1958, she took an extended thirty-day vacation to Alaska and was so enamored with the beautiful landscapes that she returned to Indiana, packed up her belongings and moved to an area near Wasilla, Alaska.

Throughout Mahala's life, she had faced racism and discrimination, and when she arrived in Alaska, she ran headlong into them once again. She was looking for some property that she could homestead, and when she arrived at the probate office, the woman manning the counter had a book of plat maps open. When she saw Mahala, she quickly tucked the book under the counter and told her that there were no properties available. A young white man who was sitting in the office overheard the conversation and asked the woman: "Why not show her the property near Wasilla that you showed me?" The woman behind the counter was outraged; she turned beet red with anger, pulled the book back out, slammed it down on the counter and walked out of the room.[4]

Eventually, Mahala homesteaded 160 acres of land just outside of Wasilla, and despite adversity, she opened two successful law offices, one in Wasilla and the other in Anchorage. She once said, "My zeal was often resented by opposing counsel. I had no fear of the other attorney and often incurred his wrath."[5] Her most notable trial victory in Alaska was a case involving the female faculty members at the University of Alaska, who were suing the institution for paying women lower wages then men.

Dickerson had a deep and abiding love for the teachings and principles of the Religious Society of Friends (Quakers), which also guided her principles when it came to righting injustice. She was the founder of the Alaska Friends Conference. Her longtime friend and neighbor Jan Bronson said that Dickerson had a simple life philosophy: "'By God we're going to fix things.'...She was spiritual and was not going to wait around on her quest for greater justice."[6]

Mahala Dickerson was honored by many groups and law associations over the years for her work. Most notably, she received the Margaret Brent Award, which was presented to her by the American Bar Association in 1995, recognizing her as an outstanding female lawyer.

Mahala Ashley Dickerson passed away in 2007 at the age of ninety-four, but her legacy continues. The Religious Society of Friends has purchased her property in Alaska and is working to create the Dickerson Center, with the hopes of continuing her legacy for years to come.

---

1. "Montgomery Industrial School for Girls," Encyclopedia of Alabama, May 4, 2007, https://encyclopediaofalabama.org.
2. Maria Downey, "Video Vault: Alaskan Civil Rights Champion Mahala Ashley Dickerson," WSAZ Video Vault, February 16, 2023, https://www.wsaz.com.
3. Downey, "Alaskan Civil Rights Champion."
4. Downey, "Alaskan Civil Rights Champion."
5. "Mahala Ashley Dickerson," National Park Service, August 7, 2021, https://www.nps.gov.
6. Christopher Cuthrell, "Who Was Mahala Ashley Dickerson?" Quaker Speak, April 1, 2021, https://quakerspeak.com.

Chapter 14

VIRGINIA FOSTER DURR

Defender of Justice and Civil Rights

Some believe that children are colorblind—that is, they don't recognize racial differences, and if left to simply be children, they don't see a person as the color of their skin. Surely, that was true for Virginia Foster, who grew up in the Jim Crow South. Her experiences as a seven-year-old in Birmingham shaped her life and career and made her a leading voice in defending civil rights and fighting injustice.

Born in Birmingham in 1903 to Dr. Sterling and Ann Foster, Virginia was an outspoken child who would defend her Black friends no matter what, as evidenced by an incident that occurred on her seventh birthday. Virginia had been ill with typhoid fever the previous year, and during her recuperation, she made plans for her upcoming birthday. In her eyes, it would be a grand party with a pink birthday cake, and she would wear a pink dress. That summer, the family traveled to their favorite vacation destination, Union Springs, Alabama, where they planned to throw Virginia her dream birthday party. Virginia didn't know many, if any, of the white children in town but was friends with several Black children, including the daughter of her Black nanny.

The trouble began when her mother and aunts told her that only white children could attend, children from the small town she didn't know. Virginia was so angry and pitched such a fit that her mother finally agreed to have a barbecue in the afternoon in the backyard, which her Black friends could attend, and then have her birthday party in the front yard with only the white children.

In attendance at the afternoon barbecue was Virginia's nanny, whom they called Nursie, and her daughter. Virginia's cousin Elizabeth was also in attendance. Nursie's daughter, who was busy tearing up barbecued chicken to fill plates with, offered a piece to Elizabeth. Elizabeth was outraged and shouted, "Don't give me any chicken out of that Black hand of yours. I'm not going to eat any chicken that your Black hand had touched, you n——."[1]

Virginia's response to her cousin was swift and to the point, telling her cousin, "Go to hell!" Her family put her to bed as punishment and told her she was going to hell for what she said. Later that afternoon, Virginia came outside for the party in the front yard and was so angry that her Black friends couldn't attend that she bashed the cake in and was sent to bed again. At the dinner table, her aunt told her mother that she was "such a bad child." Virginia was sitting there listening to her and threw her knife at her aunt.[2]

Virginia Foster eventually graduated high school and began taking college courses at Wellesley College in Massachusetts. Family financial issues forced her to leave school, but her time at the college helped further shape her outlook on life and the injustices being forced on Blacks and the poor in the South. Returning to Alabama, she married a young attorney from Montgomery, Clifford Durr, in 1926, and soon after, the couple moved to Washington, D.C. Clifford took a job working on New Deal initiatives in the Roosevelt administration, while Virginia became active in the Junior League and the Red Cross. It was at this time that Virginia learned how dairy farmers were pouring unsold milk down gutters to dispose of it. It was Virginia who convinced the Junior League to work with the farmers and have the milk donated to the poor.[3]

In 1938, Virginia became a founding member of the Southern Conference on Human Welfare, an organization that sought to promote social justice, civil rights and electoral reform in the South. The organization's first meeting was held on November 22, 1938, in Birmingham, with First Lady Eleanor Roosevelt in attendance. Black and white participants mingled freely that night, but when word of the races mixing reached city commissioner Eugene Connor—later known as the infamous "Bull" Connor who used firehoses and police dogs to attack peaceful protestors in 1963—he ordered that the meeting needed to segregate or shut down. The following night, the organization and its members complied: the races sat on opposite sides of the meeting room, but the First Lady defiantly took a seat among Black attendees.[4] That same year, Virginia approached Eleanor Roosevelt once again, and the two advocated for the elimination of poll taxes, which were a prerequisite to vote in the South.

Virginia also worked on labor issues with individuals who were labeled communists and socialists. In 1954, she was called to testify on Capitol Hill during a subcommittee hearing on communist activities. Virginia refused to name anyone as a communist and would not answer any of the committee's questions.[5] When the hearings were over, Virginia said, "In a way, I'm glad that my cover as a nice proper Southern lady was blown by the hearing because…I could begin to say what I really thought."[6]

Despite the accusations hurled at Virginia by the Senate subcommittee, she continued her work advocating for civil rights, and in July 1955, she arranged a scholarship for Rosa Parks to study at the Highlander Folk School, which was founded to teach adult education classes but, by 1950, was turning its attention to the matter of race relations.[7] Five months later, on December 1, Parks was arrested for refusing to give up her seat to a white woman on a Montgomery city bus. The night of Parks's arrest, Clifford and Virginia Durr, along with their acquaintance E.D. Nixon, bailed Rosa Parks out of jail and provided legal counsel for her. Virginia Durr, who was called by the *Atlanta Constitution* the "white matron of the civil rights movement," urged white men and women to participate in and support the Montgomery Bus Boycott. She continued her work for civil and human rights until her death in 1999. Of Virginia Foster Durr's passing, President Bill Clinton said, "Her courage, outspokenness, and steely conviction in the earliest days of the civil rights movement helped change this nation forever."[8]

---

1. Virginia Foster Durr, "Interview with Virginia Foster Durr, March 13, 14, 15, 1975. Interview G-0023-1. Southern Oral History Program Collection (#4007)," interviewed by Sue Thrasher and Jacquelyn Hall, Documenting the American South, University of North Carolina at Chapel Hill, 25–27, https://docsouth.unc.edu/sohp/G-0023-1/G-0023-1.html.
2. Durr, "Interview."
3. "Virginia Foster Durr (1903–1999)," Alabama Women's Hall of Fame, http://www.awhf.org.
4. Sam Walker, "Eleanor Roosevelt Integrates Birmingham, Alabama, Meeting," Today in Civil Liberties History, https://todayinclh.com.
5. "Virginia Foster Durr," Alabama Women's Hall of Fame.
6. Virginia Foster Durr, *Freedom Writer: Letters from the Civil Rights Years* (University of Georgia Press, 2003), 31.
7. "Highlander Folk School," Martin Luther King Jr. Research and Education Institute, Stanford University, https://kinginstitute.stanford.edu.
8. "Virginia Foster Durr," Alabama Women's Hall of Fame.

Chapter 15

GEORGIA GILMORE

Feeding a Movement

We all know the names of the civil rights icons who stood up against segregation in Montgomery, Alabama, during the yearlong Montgomery Bus Boycott of 1955, most notably Rosa Parks and Martin Luther King Jr. But there were many more who participated in the boycott but remained virtually nameless as they assisted the protestors and the cause through clandestine operations. One of those whom many say played just as important a role in the boycott as Rosa Parks was Georgia Gilmore. There were many reasons why those who supported the boycott did so in the shadows. As Georgia told author Stewart Burns for his book *Daybreak of Freedom*, "Some colored folks or Negroes could afford to stick out their necks more than others because they had independent incomes. Some just couldn't afford to be called 'ringleaders' and have the white folks fire them."[1]

Georgia Gilmore was born on a small farm in Montgomery on February 5, 1920. She would become the mother of six children, support her mother and help her mother raise her youngest sister and a niece, all while working as a cook and a midwife. Later on, her résumé would also come to include "activist." Her role as an activist for civil rights began, as many others' did, on December 1, 1955, when forty-two-year-old Rosa Parks refused to give up her seat in the white section of a Montgomery city bus and was arrested and charged with "refusing to obey the orders of the bus driver."[2] The news spread across the city like wildfire, as Georgia later recalled: "I was cooking and they made the announcement. And I didn't believe it, so I ran out and I called the lady next door…and she told me yes, it was true. And so they decided then that they would have a meeting."[3]

After Parks's arrest, it was decided that a mass meeting would be held the following Monday at seven o'clock in the evening at the Hope Street Baptist Church. During the meeting, attendees agreed that Montgomery's Black residents would no longer ride the city buses until bus segregation was made illegal. At first, it was unclear how many people would participate in the boycott. The Black community in the city relied on the buses for their livelihood; many of them worked as maids and cooks and couldn't afford other forms of transportation. They virtually kept the buses running. Doubts about how many would attend that first meeting were quickly laid to rest. The church was filled to capacity; many had to stand outside. At that moment, Georgia decided that she needed to put her skills as an incredible cook to work.

Along with some friends, Georgia established the Club from Nowhere. Its mission was to sell food to raise money to help protestors meet their needs. Regular meetings were held to organize and plan strategies. Georgia sold fried chicken sandwiches during the meetings. The club spread out across the city, selling and delivering food to beauty parlors, barbershops, laundromats, cab stands and churches. They would stop anywhere and everywhere to sell pound cakes, sweet potato pies, fried fish and stewed greens, pork chops and rice. Local Black radio stations read announcements throughout the day promoting the club's sales, with catch lines like, "Aren't you hungry? Why not buy a pie from the ladies of the boycott?"[4]

Every week, the Club from Nowhere raised between $500 and $600, all of which was used to provide alternative transportation to help workers get to their jobs and to pay for gas for carpooling, insurance and more. The boycott severely damaged the Montgomery city transportation system. Georgia told a reporter that "it was just the idea that you could make the white man suffer and let the white man realize that you could get along in the world without him."[5]

It didn't take long for Georgia's home to become a meeting place as well. People would stop in and buy one of her incredible meals—and it wasn't just average people from around the city. Her home played host to the Reverend Martin Luther King Jr., who was a regular and became practically a part of her family (King called her "Tiny"); the Reverend Ralph Abernathy; and extra-special guests invited by King, including Robert F. Kennedy and Lyndon Johnson.[6]

Finally, on November 13, 1956, the U.S. Supreme Court upheld a lower court's ruling that Montgomery's bus segregation law violated the Fourteenth Amendment. The boycott continued, however, for another month until the verdict was officially in the hands of Montgomery city officials. On December 20, 1956, just over one year since the boycott began, Reverend King made the announcement: the boycott was over. The following morning, Reverend King and Reverend Abernathy climbed aboard the first desegregated bus in Montgomery.

Georgia recalled the moment the boycott ended:

> *I was glad because we discovered that we had a lot of white friends that we didn't realize...were interested in us, and the only reason that they couldn't let it be known publicly before the boycott was because they thought that maybe they would be isolated from their white friends. So after the boycott...they found that we had so many white friends,* [and] *then they could let it be known that they were really and truly interested in you as a human being, not of your color, but as a human being.*[7]

Georgia Gilmore's role as an unsung hero of the Montgomery Bus Boycott was not known for many years outside of the city, but today, history has opened its book for her. Journalist Safiya Charles eloquently summed up Georgia's life in one line: "She used food as a weapon and a salve."[8]

---

1. Clancey Miller, "Overlooked No More: Georgia Gilmore Who Fed and Funded the Montgomery Bus Boycott," *New York Times*, July 31, 2019.
2. "An Act of Courage, the Arrest Records of Rosa Parks," National Archives, December 21, 2016, https://www.archives.gov.
3. "Eyes on the Prize; Interview with Georgia Gilmore," American Archive of Public Broadcasting (GBH and the Library of Congress), http://americanarchive.org/catalog/cpb-aacip-151-bv79s1mb8s.
4. Davia Nelson and Nikki Silva, "A Secret Civil Rights Kitchen: Georgia Gilmore and the Club from Nowhere," *The Kitchen Sisters Present* (podcast), Radiotopia, https://kitchensisters.org.
5. "Interview with Georgia Gilmore," American Archive of Public Broadcasting.
6. Nelson and Silva, "Secret Civil Rights Kitchen"; "Interview with Georgia Gilmore," American Archive of Public Broadcasting.
7. "Interview with Georgia Gilmore," American Archive of Public Broadcasting.
8. Southern Foodways Alliance, "Lessons from Georgia Gilmore," YouTube, October 27, 2021, https://youtu.be/tQ062SsBTIQ.

Chapter 16

DIXIE BIBB GRAVES

Alabama's First Woman Senator

Dixie Bibb Graves left her mark on society as a civic leader, playing active roles in the Woman's Christian Temperance Union (WCTU), the Alabama Federation of Women's Clubs, the Alabama Historical Society, the Women's Missionary Union of the First Christian Church and the Young Women's Christian Association (YWCA). Throughout her life, she advocated for child labor laws and literacy programs, but what she is most remembered for is serving as the first female senator from Alabama.

Dixie—or Miss Dixie, as friends called her—was born in Montgomery on July 26, 1882, and lived there virtually all her life. She came from a distinguished line of Alabama politicians, most notably William Wyatt Bibb and Thomas Bibb, the first two governors of Alabama. When she turned eighteen, Dixie married her first cousin, state legislator Bibb Graves. Bibb was on the fast track in politics but would not work in the legislature for long. Running as a New Deal Democrat, her husband was elected governor of the state not once but twice, in 1927 and again in 1935. His wife, Dixie, played a key role in his campaign for Alabama's top political seat. During his campaigns, if Bibb couldn't attend a rally, Dixie addressed the crowd for him. As the *Montgomery Advertiser* described her, she was a woman with "a keen intelligence and amazing grasp of national problems."[1]

Dixie became a staunch supporter of the women's suffrage movement, and in 1919, she addressed the state legislature, urging representatives to ratify the Nineteenth Amendment.[2] The amendment was rejected on September 22, 1919, and would not be ratified by the state until September 8, 1953.[3]

The lady from Alabama in Washington, D.C., November 13, 1937: Alabama's first female senator, Dixie Bibb Graves. *Library of Congress, Prints and Photographs Division.*

Undaunted, Dixie continued pushing for women's right to vote, and one year after her address to the Alabama statehouse, she became a founding member of the Alabama League of Women Voters.

In 1937, Dixie made her way to Washington, D.C., when a serving U.S. senator from Alabama, Hugo L. Black, was appointed to the U.S. Supreme Court by President Roosevelt. With the backing of FDR and Hugo Black, Bibb Graves appointed his wife to fill the vacant seat until a special election could be held, making her the first female senator from Alabama. As Graves was a junior member of the Senate, her desk was located in the very back of the chamber in what was called the Cherokee Strip, a sort of no-man's-land in the Senate where new members had to sit. The seats were located between both parties, hence the name Cherokee Strip, alluding to a section of land in Oklahoma that did not belong to either the United States government or Indian Territory.

On taking the seat, as the drumbeat of the United States entering a war in Europe grew louder, Dixie introduced her first piece of legislation, a law that would conscript all natural resources to the federal government during times of war. It would also make it mandatory for women to be drafted into military service as well as men. The proposed legislation died in committee.[4]

Graves also made history when she became the first woman to address the Senate. It was very rare for a new member to address the chamber and unheard of for a woman to do so. Dixie spoke for twenty minutes on the Senate floor opposing an anti-lynching law. While she told senators that she deplored the crime, the matter, she said, should be left up to the states to decide.[5] Dixie Bibb Graves did not run for reelection, and only five months after her appointment, she resigned her seat after Lister Hill won the state's special election. Though short, her time in the U.S. Senate was historic in many ways.

---

1. "Dixie Bibb Graves (1883–1965)," Alabama Women's Hall of Fame, http://www.awhf.org.
2. Hattie Engel Kaufman, "Biographical Sketch of Dixie Bibb Graves," included in Women and Social Movements, Part III: Mainstream Suffragists, Alexander Street, https://documents.alexanderstreet.com/d/1010596119.
3. "19th Amendment by State," National Park Service, July 22, 2020, https://www.nps.gov.
4. Kaufman, "Dixie Bibb Graves."
5. Kaufman, "Dixie Bibb Graves."

Chapter 17

ADELE "VERA" HALL

Singing from a Source of Gold and Light

It was a cool spring day in the rural Sumter County town of Paynesville, Alabama, when Adele Hall was born. Little did her parents know that the young girl they held in their arms would be recognized as the nation's foremost singer of the blues and African American spirituals.[1] If it weren't for the efforts of the Works Progress Administration's (WPA) Federal Writers' Project, her incredible voice might never have been heard outside of Sumter County and lost forever.

Adele's mother, Agnes, was a former slave. Her father, Efron "Zully" Hall, was a Baptist preacher. Adele was taught gospel singing at an early age and became well known throughout the community. In 1918, Adele, who was better known as Vera, married Nels Riddle, a coal miner, and soon gave birth to their daughter, Minnie. Tragically, Nash was killed in a fight, and Adele had to fend for herself and her daughter, becoming a cook, nursemaid and washerwoman.[2]

In 1937, Alabama folklorist Ruby Pickens Tartt was assigned a task by the Roosevelt administration's Federal Writers' Project to document spiritual singers in the South. Being from Sumter County herself, Tartt knew of Vera and recorded her. She then shared the recordings with John Lomax, a musicologist and folk music preservationist, who immediately fell in love with Vera's voice. "The sound comes from deep within her when she sings," Lomax later told *Sing Out!* magazine in an interview, "from a source of gold and light, otherwise hidden, and falls directly upon your ear like sunlight."[3]

Lomax recorded Vera for the Library of Congress several times between 1937 and 1940, sometimes performing spiritual duets with her cousin, Doc Reed. While Reed called the blues the "Devil's music," Vera, on the other hand, embraced the style. She leaned more heavily into singing the blues and away from spiritual songs after the passing of her mother. "I don't sing 'um around nobody," she told Lomax, as he later recalled in his book *The Rainbow Sign*. "I go off in the kitchen and close the door before I sing a blues that fits my case."[4]

Vera was recorded yet again in 1945 by University of Alabama professor Byron Arnold. While Vera never did become a professional singer, she did appear at the American Music Festival at New York's Columbia University on May 15, 1948. She passed away in 1964 at age sixty-two in Tuscaloosa. And while she never did become a recording sensation and her name isn't well known, her sound still resonates in those few recordings made by Lomax and the WPA, which can still be heard today on the Library of Congress and Smithsonian Museum websites.[5]

---

1. "Adele 'Vera' Hall," Encyclopedia of Alabama, January 1, 2007, https://encyclopediaofalabama.org.
2. "Biography: Vera Hall (1902–1964)," Library of Congress, https://www.loc.gov.
3. "Vera Ward Hall: April 6, 1902–January 29, 1964," Lomax Digital Archive, https://archive.culturalequity.org.
4. Alan Lomax, *The Rainbow Sign* (Duell, Sloan and Pearce, 1959), 103.
5. Dock Reed and Vera Hall Ward, *Spirituals with Dock Reed and Vera Hall Ward* (Folkways Records, 1953), Smithsonian Folkways Recordings, https://folkways.si.edu.

Chapter 18

MIA HAMM

Going for the Goal

Mariel Margaret Hamm, better known as Mia Hamm, is undoubtedly the greatest female soccer player of all time, with a career that helped spark American interest in a sport few took notice of at the time and created what ESPN called Mia Mania.[1] But don't tell Mia she's the greatest. As she humbly wrote in her 1999 book *Go for the Goal*, "Many people say I'm the best woman's soccer player in the world. I don't think so and because of that, someday I just might be."[2]

Mia was born in Selma, Alabama, on March 17, 1972, the third of Bill and Stephanie Hamm's four daughters. She was nicknamed Mia by her mother, who once studied under ballerina Mia Slavenska. Her father was a U.S. Air Force colonel, and the family traveled with him around the world to various duty stations. In 1977, Bill and Stephanie adopted a newborn baby, Mia's brother Garrett. As he grew older, young Garrett developed a passion for sports, a passion he shared with his older sister.

Mia became a soccer fan early on, as a toddler, when she would sit and be mesmerized by watching the game on television and then head outside to kick the ball in the backyard. Eventually, she played soccer in high school, and at the age of fourteen, she was noticed by the coach of the national soccer team, Anson Dorrance, while she was playing in a tournament in Louisiana. At first, the coach was a little skeptical about her talent. "I didn't ask who she was. I wanted to let her emerge," Dorrance told ESPN. "This skinny brunette accelerated to the ball like she'd been shot out of a cannon. I'd never seen athleticism like that. I ran around screaming, 'Is that Mia Hamm?'"[3] At the age of fifteen, Mia became the youngest ever member of the U.S. national team. She was now on the fast track to becoming a sports legend.

In 1989, Mia began college at the University of North Carolina–Charlotte (UNC), where she played forward for the Tar Heels. By the time she graduated, she had helped the team win four NCAA championships.[4] In addition, she was named the All-American and ACC Player of the Year for three consecutive years and finished her ACC career as the all-time leading scorer in goals (103), assists (72) and points (278).[5]

In 1991, she helped the U.S. national team win the Women's World Cup, repeating the feat again in 1999. On May 22, 1999, during the run-up to the 1999 World Cup final match, Mia scored her 108th international goal in a game against Brazil, breaking the record previously held by Elisabetta Vignotto of Italy.[6] In all, Mia played in four World Cups.

Between World Cup wins, Olympic gold was calling, and Mia and the U.S. Women's Olympic Soccer team didn't disappoint, capturing gold in 1999 and 2000 and silver in 2004. The talent Mia showed on the field earned her the Women's World Player of the Year award from the Fédération Internationale de Football Association (FIFA) in 2001 and 2002.

Mia officially retired from the sport in 2004 with 158 goals in international competition, the most by any male or female player at the time. One year earlier, after moving to Los Angeles, she married Major League Baseball shortstop Nomar Garciaparra, and soon after, the couple became the parents of twin girls.

But Mia's story is about more than just soccer. Her brother, Garrett, suffered from a rare and serious blood condition, aplastic anemia. The condition occurs when your bone marrow cannot make enough new blood cells for your body to function normally.[7] After receiving a bone marrow transplant, Garrett developed Graft-Versus-Host Disease (GVHD). Occasionally, during an organ transplant, the recipient's body rejects the organ. In GVHD, the opposite occurs: the donor's cells attack the recipient's organs and tissues.[8] Tragically, Garrett passed away at age twenty-eight in 1997. Two years later, in honor of her brother, Mia founded the Mia Hamm Foundation, a nonprofit dedicated to raising awareness and funds for families in need of a marrow or cord blood transplant.[9]

When it comes to the soccer career of Mia Hamm, no one summed it up better than soccer legend Pele, who wrote, "When I was playing they said soccer was a man's world and that a woman should remain on the sidelines. All I can say is that I'm glad I never had to go up against Mia Hamm."[10]

---

1. Lisette Hilton, "No Me in Mia," ESPN Classic, https://www.espn.com/classic/biography/s/Hamm_Mia.html.
2. Mia Hamm and Aaron Heifetz, *Go for the Goal: A Champion's Guide to Winning in Soccer and Life* (Quill, 1999), 3.
3. Hilton, "No Me in Mia."
4. "Mia Hamm," International Olympic Committee, https://olympics.com.
5. "Inductees: Mia Hamm," Alabama Sports Hall of Fame, August 2, 2019, https://ashof.org.
6. "Mia Hamm," International Olympic Committee.
7. "Anemia: Aplastic Anemia," National Heart, Lung, and Blood Institute, March 24, 2022, https://www.nhlbi.nih.gov.
8. "What Is Graft-Versus-Host Disease (GVHD)?" GVHD Now, https://www.gvhdnow.com.
9. Mia Hamm Foundation, https://www.miafoundation.org.
10. Hamm, *Go for the Goal*, back cover.

Chapter 19

EMMYLOU HARRIS

A Red Dirt Girl from a Red Dirt Town

One of the most respected singer/songwriters in country music is Birmingham native Emmylou Harris. In a career that has spanned over four decades, she's amassed quite a catalog of music, having recorded twenty-five albums and countless duets, received accolades and admiration from musicians in all genres of music and amassed a warehouse full of awards.

Harris was born in Birmingham in 1947 to Eugenia and Walter Harris. Her father was a U.S. Marine Corps pilot who served in both World War II and the Korean War. He was shot down and captured during the Korean conflict, but when he returned to the United States, he remained on active duty and became the presidential command pilot for U.S. presidents from Eisenhower to Carter.[1]

Harris was a "military brat," and her family moved around the country many times, including stops in Washington, D.C., and North Carolina. After graduating high school as class valedictorian with a 4.0 GPA, she attended college at the University of North Carolina, where she studied drama.

Emmylou had a fondness for urban folk groups, and in 1969, she tried her hand at the genre, recording an album titled *Gliding Bird.* The album was not a resounding success, but it did boost her notoriety locally. Her introduction to country music came by way of an acquaintance she made with singer/songwriter Graham Parsons. Parsons had been a member of the 1960s groups the Byrds and the Flying Burrito Brothers. To this day, Emmylou credits Parsons with helping her realize the powerful resonance of country music through their work together. The harmonization between Parsons and Harris is powerful and touches one's soul. She said in an interview:

> *I did approach what I consider to be the real beginning of my musical apprenticeship becoming a true musician and artist from the point of view of a harmony singer, and that was from singing with Graham. I think he was able to take the love of traditional country music which is a powerful musical form and combine it with a real sense of rock 'n roll poetry. But he was unabashedly passionate about country music.*[2]

It was her incredible harmonies that made her one of the most beloved and admired singers in the music industry and have kept her in high demand, recording duets with the likes of Bryan Adams, Beck, Elvis Costello, Johnny Cash, Lucinda Williams, Bob Dylan, Tammy Wynette, Neil Young, the Chieftains, Lyle Lovett, Roy Orbison, the Band, Willie Nelson, George Jones—and the list keeps on going.

Her own solo success began in 1975 when she released the album *Pieces of the Sky*, with the hit single "If I Could Only Win Your Love." The single reached No. 4 on the Billboard Country Singles Chart and became a certified gold record. Her second album, *Elite Hotel* (released in 1976), won her the Best Female Country Vocal Performance award at the 1976 Grammy Awards. It would be her first of thirteen Grammys, with forty-seven nominations.[3] Since then, she has recorded over twenty-five albums, which have sold over fifteen million copies.

From there, the awards and accolades continued. She was inducted into the Country Music Hall of Fame in 2008, won the Grammy Lifetime Achievement Award in 2018 and won the 2015 Polar Music Award. In making the announcement via video, the organization described her talent this way: "No one in the history of popular music has harmonized like Emmylou Harris....But it is [as] an artist in her own right that she has made the greatest contribution....Her voice follows the contours of the American landscape, from the highest peaks to the endless prairies."[4]

Emmylou has used her fame and talents to advocate for many worthy causes. Since 1997, she has been a spokesperson for the International Campaign to Ban Landmines. She is also an animal rights activist and founder of Boneparte's Retreat, an organization that rescues pets for Metro Nashville Animal Care and Control.

Emmylou Harris: just a red dirt girl from a red dirt town who is humble about her success. "I'm blessed to be able to work at something that I'm good at, and that I love," she says. "It's not something I take for granted."[5]

1. "Famous Brats: Emmylou Harris, Singer / Songwriter," American Overseas Schools Historical Society, October 12, 2015, https://aoshs.org.
2. Emmylou Harris, in discussion with the author, January 1991.
3. "Artist: Emmylou Harris," Grammy Awards, https://www.grammy.com.
4. "2015 Laureate Emmylou Harris," Polar Music Prize, https://www.polarmusicprize.org/laureates/emmylou-harris.
5. "Artist: Emmylou Harris," Grammy Awards.

Chapter 20

DONNA HILLEY

A Force to Reckon With in the Country Music Industry

Whether you like country music or not, you may know the big names that made the genre what it is today: Conway Twitty, Tammy Wynette, Merle Haggard. But those are the faces of country music. Behind the scenes, there was one woman who helped shaped the country music world as we know it today: Montevallo, Alabama native Donna Hilley.

The daughter of John Truman "Whitt" Whitten and Janie Mae Whitten, Donna attended Jones Valley Elementary School in Birmingham after the family moved there for her father's job with the Alabama Power Company. It was in eighth grade that her future husband, Rayford Hilley, first set eyes on her, and the couple knew right from the start that this was a love that would last forever. Rayford was two years older than Donna and was the captain of the school's football team. In an interview with the *Birmingham News*, Rayford said that when he first saw her, she was "beating the stew out of some boy." Donna agreed, replying, "I used to beat up everybody. You might say I was a tomboy. The first time I wore stockings, I climbed a tree."[1]

When Rayford graduated high school, he left for Nashville to attend college and play football at Vanderbilt University. After Donna's graduation in 1958, she left the Magic City to join her boyfriend, and they were married soon after. Still a teenager, Donna began working at WKDA radio in Nashville as a receptionist. The station's program director was Jack Stapp. Stapp had, at one time, been the program director of WSM radio in Nashville, the station that brought the Grand Ol' Opry to the world every weekend. While at WSM, in 1958, Stapp asked songwriter Buddy Killen to find him some songs that he could publish. One of those songs was "Heartbreak Hotel," which was recorded by Elvis Presley. It was the beginning of a monumental publishing company, Tree Publishing, later to be known as Tree International.[2]

Meanwhile, Donna left her job at WKDA and began working at an advertising agency, where she quickly rose up the chain of command. After working at the agency for several years, in 1978, Donna received a phone call from her old boss, Jack Stapp. Stapp told Hilley that his secretary was ill and that there was only one person who could do her job. And with that, Hilley joined Tree Publishing as the executive vice president and chief operating officer, working her way up to president and chief executive officer by 1998.[3]

Donna Hilley was responsible for making Tree International the major player it is in the industry, broadening its scope from just country music to Broadway musicals, movies and television. She was the first to blend country and Christian music, a trend that filled the airwaves with hit after hit in the 1990s.[4] In 1989, Hilley brokered a deal with Sony Corporation in which the media giant purchased Tree International. In 1994, she was made the CEO of Sony ATV in Nashville. In her role as CEO, she made Sony/ATV a huge financial success as she secured the song catalogs of such country greats as Acuff-Rose (which included hit songs like the Everly Brothers' "When Will I Be Loved" and "Bye, Bye Love"), Conway Twitty, Buck Owens and Merle Haggard, to name only a few.[5]

For her work, Donna was named Woman of the Year by the Business and Professional Women's Club in 1978. In 1992, she was ranked the fourth most powerful woman in country music by *Entertainment Weekly*, and in 1994, she became the first woman elected to the board of directors of the American Society of Composers, Authors and Artists (ASCAP). She also served on the board of the National Academy of Recording Arts and Sciences. Her most cherished award came in 1999 when she was inducted into the Alabama Music Hall of Fame. "Of all the things I've accomplished, this means the most," she told the *Birmingham News*. "I'm just glad they did it while I'm still living and can enjoy it."[6]

Donna Hilley passed away on June 20, 2012, following a long illness. The president and CEO of Sony ATV at the time of her passing, Troy Thomlinson, best summarized Donna's incredible career:

> *Donna Hilley's influence on Music Row's artists and songwriters and on the broader Nashville community could never fully be expressed with words. She was an icon in every sense—an inspiring trailblazer for women executives in the music business, a staunch advocate for artists and songwriters and a genuine competitor who was respected, but never underestimated, by her peers.*[7]

---

1. Kathy Kemp, "Kathy Kemp's 1999 Interview with Donna Hilley in the *Birmingham News*," *Birmingham News*, June 21, 2012.
2. "Jack Stapp," Country Music Hall of Fame and Museum, https://www.countrymusichalloffame.org.
3. "Celebrating the Women in Alabama Music: Donna Hilley," Alabama Music Hall of Fame, https://www.alamhof.org.
4. "Donna Hilley," Alabama Music Hall of Fame.
5. Billboard Staff, "Donna Hilley, Former Sony ATV Nashville CEO, Dead at 65," Billboard, June 21, 2012, https://www.billboard.com.
6. Kemp, "Interview with Donna Hilley."
7. "Remembering Donna Hilley," BMI, June 21, 2012, https://www.bmi.com.

Chapter 21

ELLEN DORRIT HOFFLEIT

Stars in Her Eyes

As a young girl, Ellen Dorrit Hoffleit faced strong headwinds from her own mother, who believed she would never amount to much. Ellen set out to prove her mother wrong and went on to become one of the most prolific and successful astronomers in the world.

Dorrit's parents, Fred and Kate Hoffleit, were German immigrants who took up residence in Florence, Alabama. Dorrit was born in 1907, creating a bit of a conflict in the Hoffleit home. Fred wanted to name her Ellen; her mother wanted to name her Dorrit. Her official name was a combination of the two, but when it came to what she should be called, her mother won out, and everyone called her Dorrit. As Dorrit said, "The woman in the house is always right."[1]

Dorrit's own mother believed her daughter would not amount to much. For example, her older brother Herbert was considered highly intelligent, eventually graduating from Harvard with a PhD in the classics. One day, while Dorrit was taking a walk with her mother, they crossed paths with one of Dorrit's public school teachers, who remarked, "Dorrit isn't nearly as bright as her brother, is she?" Her mother replied, "What can you expect? She's only a girl."[2] Her mother's opinion even played a role in the young girl's college education. The only reason her parents sent her to Radcliffe College in Massachusetts was so that their "brilliant son wouldn't be ashamed of his dumb sister."[3] "All the hardships taught me something," Dorrit was later quoted as saying. "They taught me how to cope. So I was prepared to fight back."

Before college, the family moved to New Castle, Pennsylvania, where Dorrit's father had landed a bookkeeping job. It was here that her love of astronomy began as she turned her gaze to the stars, standing in awe, mesmerized by the Perseid meteor shower. When she started her studies at Radcliffe in 1924, she couldn't decide if she wanted to study math or art. Her decision was made when that same summer, she was offered the position of research assistant at the Harvard College Observatory. With only two basic-level astronomy courses under her belt, the young woman became an expert in spectroscopy, a method of determining the absolute brightness of stars.

Dorrit went on to earn her MA in astronomy in 1932 and went on to earn a PhD in astronomy from Harvard. She continued working at the Harvard Observatory until she accepted a job at the Ballistic Research Laboratory at the Aberdeen Proving Ground in Maryland, where she calculated missile trajectories during World War II. She returned to the Harvard Observatory in 1948, doing the same work as the men there—but she made only forty cents an hour compared to the men's one dollar. She moved on to work at Yale University in 1956, where she was named director of the Maria Mitchell Observatory in Nantucket and took over the college's star-cataloging program. It was here that she began a research program for undergraduates interested in astronomy that was attended primarily by young women. Eleven of those women went on to earn PhDs themselves and, in total, publish over ninety research papers and discover over one thousand new variable stars.

In her life, Dorrit published countless scholarly papers and was a contributor to *Sky and Telescope* magazine. And even though she retired in 1975, she continued her work until she passed away in 2007. In 1982, she authored the *Yale Bright Star Catalogue*, a volume of work that can be found in every observatory in the world, and five years later, she was honored in the most fitting way when an asteroid was named for her: Asteroid Dorrit.

---

1. Kristen Larsen, "Variable Stars and Constant Commitments: The Stellar Career of Dorrit Hoffleit," *Journal of the American Association of Variable Star Observers* 40 (2012): 44.
2. "Dorrit Hoffleit," Connecticut Women's Hall of Fame, https://www.cwhf.org.
3. Larsen, "Variable Stars," 44.

Chapter 22

PATTIE RUFFNER JACOBS

Crusader for Justice and Women's Rights

To tackle a social issue, you sometimes have to back up and look at it from a different perspective, and that was the challenge Pattie Ruffner Jacobs faced when she was fighting to reform child labor laws in the early 1900s. She realized that to make any significant inroads, she would need the backing of a large bloc of voters—the women of Alabama—who didn't yet have the right to vote. Jacobs set her sights on correcting that, dedicating her life to achieving equal voting rights in Alabama.

Pattie Belle Ruffner was born in West Virginia to Lewis and Virginia Ruffner on October 2, 1875, the youngest of six children. The family moved to Nashville, where their father operated a highly successful mercantile business. There, Pattie attended school at Ward Seminary (now Belmont University), from which she graduated in 1893. That same year, her parents separated. Along with her mother and siblings, Pattie moved to Birmingham, where she continued her education at the Birmingham Training School for Teachers before heading off to New York City, where she studied humanities. She returned to Birmingham in 1898, and that's when her activism began to take shape.

On returning to the Magic City, Pattie met a rich businessman, Solon "Sol" Jacobs, a man ten years older than herself. The couple married that same year and eventually had two daughters. Solon's financial success with the Birmingham Slag Company made it possible for Pattie to volunteer for her many pet passions and advocate for a number of causes, including reforming child labor laws; championing workers' rights, including advocating for the eight-hour workday; and supporting the banning of convict leasing, a means

Pattie Jacobs, president of the Alabama Suffrage Association, circa 1913. *Library of Congress.*

of filling the labor void in the South following the abolition of slavery by imprisoning Black men, women and children who had been arrested for minor offenses and then leasing them out to private businesses.[1]

Now, you have to remember that this was a time when most husbands would not allow their wives to participate in politics or advocate for social issues outside of the home, but Solon was a unique man for the time and backed Pattie's efforts 100 percent. With his steady backing and financial support, she set out to make a change in the world—but she quickly realized that to make any difference, women would need to be part of the solution, so she took up the crusade to obtain the right to vote for women. She began making speeches for suffrage across the state, sponsored suffrage meetings and published numerous pamphlets and flyers promoting the cause. She encouraged women to speak out openly and freely for their rights and on behalf of those who were not permitted to even read suffrage literature or attend meetings. She also encouraged those who could speak out to use what was called "voiceless speech," where women would stand in a shop window with suffrage literature in their hands, holding it up so that women passing by could read it, making it look like they were simply window shopping.[2]

Pattie's work with the suffrage movement took a giant leap forward when, in 1911, she founded the Birmingham Equal Suffrage Association and then, one year later, the Alabama Equal Suffrage Association. When she was elected president of the Alabama association, she became the youngest officeholder in any suffrage organization in the nation.

Pattie Ruffner Jacobs worked tirelessly to give Alabama women the right to vote, holding countless rallies and fundraising events and even organizing a Suffrage Day at Rickwood Field, home of the Southern League minor league baseball team, the Birmingham Barons. Eventually, she accumulated over one hundred thousand signatures on a petition asking the state legislature to place a suffrage amendment on the ballot. In 1916, State Representative Jospeh Green of Selma agreed that the issue should be brought up in the statehouse and backed Jacobs, crafting legislation to provide women with this valuable right. When the bill came to a vote, however, it was defeated 52 to 43. What's ironic is that even the bill's sponsor, Green, voted against it.[3]

After the death of the bill, Pattie joined the National American Woman Suffrage Association in 1916 and became one of the movement's most dedicated and powerful speakers.[4] The national organization dispatched her on nationwide speaking tours until the Nineteenth Amendment to the Constitution was passed on August 20, 1920. After its passing, Pattie said, "And now by the thousands we have worked out our own salvation, and we have unshackled ourselves spiritually. We are not bound or gagged by any tradition which thwarts justice. Justice has become our tradition just as to all the hitherto unprivileged."[5]

When the amendment was ratified nationally—except in Alabama, which did not ratify it until 1953—Pattie transformed the Alabama Equal Suffrage Association into the Alabama League of Women Voters (ALWV) and was eventually appointed secretary of the national LWV. The mission of the organization was to prepare women for their newfound responsibility as full citizens.

Pattie Ruffner Jacobs continued to play an important role in social issues facing Alabama and serve as a role model for political action not only in the state but nationally as well. President Woodrow Wilson tapped her to promote buying liberty bonds during World War I; President Franklin Roosevelt made her head of the women's division of the Consumer Advisory Board of the National Recovery Administration (NRA); and she was appointed to be the first National Democratic Committeewoman from Alabama and sat on the National Democratic Committee, a position she held until her death in 1935.[6] She was inducted into the Alabama Women's Hall of Fame in 1978.

---

1. "Pattie Ruffner Jacobs (1875–1935)," Alabama Women's Hall of Fame, http://www.awhf.org.
2. "Pattie Ruffner Jacobs," Encyclopedia of Alabama, March 13, 2007, https://encyclopediaofalabama.org.
3. Alex Colvin, "Pattie Ruffner Jacobs, Suffragist," Alabama Department of Archives & History, YouTube, November 22, 2024, https://youtu.be/okwNRcG8VK0.
4. Alabama Public Television, "Pattie Ruffner Jacobs: They Dared!" YouTube, November 22, 2024, https://youtu.be/r5dSPRdreuY.
5. Colvin, "Pattie Ruffner Jacobs."
6. "Pattie Ruffner Jacobs," Alabama Women's Hall of Fame.

Chapter 23

MAE JEMISON

Reaching for the Stars and Beyond

"Strange, but I always knew I'd be here. Looking down and all around me, seeing the Earth, the moon, and the stars, I just felt that I belonged right there, and in fact, any place in the entire universe."[1]

Mae Jemison really did belong in the stars, as she wrote in her book, *Find Where the Wind Goes: Moments from My Life*, about floating above the Earth aboard the International Space Station. One could say her entire life led up to the moment when she became the first African American woman in space, but there is much more to Dr. Jemison than her time spent in space.

Mae was born in Decatur, Alabama, on October 17, 1956, to Charlie and Dorothy Jemison. Her father was a maintenance supervisor, her mother a teacher, and both encouraged their young daughter to excel in her education. When Mae was three, her mother became dissatisfied with the job opportunities Alabama held for her, so the family made the decision to move to Chicago, where they had more and better options. In the Windy City, the family often spent their free time at the Chicago Museum of Science and Industry and the Field Museum. As soon as Mae could read, she obtained a library card and began checking out books about dinosaurs, evolution, the stars and the planets.

But Mae Jemison had another passion besides science: dancing. At the age of eight, she took beginning ballet, and later, when she entered college, she took modern dance, jive, swing and Brazilian dance classes. "Dance was always very important to me," she wrote, "and I believe helped me through Stanford [University]. I think it is the creativity, athleticism, musicality, and

Astronaut Mae C. Jemison, STS-47 mission specialist, appears to be clicking her heels in zero gravity in this 35mm frame photographed in the science module aboard the Earth-orbiting space shuttle *Endeavour*. *NASA*.

story narrative that must be integrated and communicated at the same time that makes dancing so invigorating and peaceful."[2]

While Mae had strong educational support from her family during her public school years, she said that some of her teachers discouraged her from pursuing an education in science. "Sometimes people want to tell you to act or to be a certain way," she wrote. "Sometimes people want to limit you because of their own limited imaginations."[3] Mae overcame those obstacles and excelled in elementary school, during which time she first learned about astronomy at the Adler Planetarium. Her high school science fair project on sickle cell anemia took first place in a citywide competition, and she remained on the school's honor roll her entire high school career, graduating in 1973 at sixteen. She attended Stanford University in California, graduating in 1977 with a Bachelor of Science degree in chemical engineering and a Bachelor of Arts in African American studies.

From there, it was off to Cornell University in New York, during which time she spent a summer in East Africa working for the African Medical and Education Research Foundation (formerly the Flying Doctors), providing medical services to people who might never see a doctor in their life. She graduated Cornell in 1981 with a doctorate in medicine and went on to intern at the Los Angeles County Medical Center before opening her own practice. She also joined the Peace Corps for a time as a medical officer.[4]

On June 18, 1983, Mae watched history in the making as astronaut Sally Ride became the first American woman in space when she launched from Cape Kennedy aboard the space shuttle *Challenger*. Mae saw her chance to reach for the stars. In 1985, she applied to NASA's astronaut training program, but one year later, tragedy struck when the same shuttle that launched Sally Ride into history, *Challenger*, exploded just after liftoff, killing all aboard. The hiring of new astronauts was put on hold until an investigation into the accident could be completed. When the program was resumed in 1987, Jemison reapplied. Out of two thousand applicants, she was selected to be one of fifteen new astronauts. Finally, on September 12, 1992, Mae Jemison made history herself when she launched as mission specialist aboard the shuttle *Endeavour* to conduct experiments over two hundred miles above the Earth on the International Space Station.

After resigning from the astronaut corps in 1993, Mae continued her work in both science and medicine, focusing on improving health care in Africa and advancing technology in developing countries through an organization she founded, the Jemison Group. She also currently leads a global initiative to ensure that capabilities for human travel beyond the solar system will exist within the next one hundred years, called the 100 Year Starship initiative.[5] Additionally, she is a prominent voice in science, technology, engineering and mathematics (STEM) education and the founder of the nonprofit Dorothy Jemison Foundation for Excellence.

---

1. Mae Jemison, *Find Where the Wind Goes: Moments from My Life* (Scholastic, 2001), 225.
2. Jemison, *Where the Wind Goes*, 148.
3. Vickie Lindsey, "She Had a Dream: Mae C. Jemison, First African American Woman in Space," National Air and Space Museum, September 12, 2010, https://airandspace.si.edu.
4. Marisa Mathis, "Mae Jemison (1956–)," National Women's History Museum, November 22, 2024, https://www.womenshistory.org.
5. "Mae Jemison: Class of 2023–2024," Hagler Institute for Advanced Study at Texas A&M University, https://hias.tamu.edu.

Chapter 24

HALLE TANNER DILLON JOHNSON

Trailblazing and Tenacious

In 1880 Alabama, history was in the making. A bill was making its way through the state legislature that would establish a college for Black students in Macon County and provide $2,000 in annual state funding. The bill was written by Lewis Adams, a former slave, and George W. Campbell, a former slaveholder. The bill passed and was signed into law on February 12, 1881, by Governor Rufus Willis Cobb. The Tuskegee Normal School for Colored Teachers, later known as the Tuskegee Institute, was born.

Originally, the state legislature suggested that the school principal be a white male, but former Union General Samuel Armstrong Chapman had another idea and recommended his friend Booker T. Washington for the position. When offered the job, Washington accepted. Washington would make a historic decision of his own in a few years: to hire the first Black female doctor in the state, Halle Tanner Dillon Johnson.

Tanner was born into a prominent Pittsburgh family in 1861. The family moved to Philadelphia, where her father, Benjamin Tucker Tanner, was a minister with the African Methodist Episcopal (AME) church. The family home was often filled with prominent African Americans, who met to discuss the political and cultural issues of the day.[1] Halle was one of nine Tanner children, and her family made sure they were all well-educated. The young woman also had a few distinguished relatives in her family tree, including her brother, Henry Ossawa Tanner, America's first great Black artist, who was known worldwide for his expressive realistic paintings, and her niece Sadie, who was the first Black woman in the United States to receive a PhD.

In 1886, Halle married Charles Dillon, and the couple moved to Trenton, New Jersey. They had one child before Charles passed away suddenly due to complications from pneumonia; Halle returned to Philadelphia to live with her parents. On returning to Philadelphia, she decided to attend college and entered the Woman's Medical College of Pennsylvania, the only Black woman in her class. Halle graduated in 1891 with her medical degree with honors.[2]

It was at this point that the path of Halle Tanner Dillon would cross with that of Booker T. Washington, who was searching for a candidate to serve as a medical doctor at Tuskegee. Washington wrote to the Woman's College asking if they had any suitable candidates. Dillon's name was submitted, and Washington offered her the position, where she would serve as pharmacist, teacher and doctor to the college's 450 students, 30 faculty members and the entire Tuskegee community. Her employer would pay her an annual salary of $600 and provide room and board.[3]

Before she could begin work, however, she had to take the Alabama medical exam. The exam was recognized around the country as one of the most stringent in the nation—or, as *The New York Times* called it, "unusually severe." It would take ten days and cover ten different subjects, administered by ten different examiners. Dr. Cornelius N. Dorsette, the first licensed and certified Black doctor in the state, volunteered to mentor Dillon as she prepared for the exam. The odds seemed stacked against her, not only because of how difficult the exam would be but also because she was a Black woman. When she told her father what she was about to get herself into, he wrote to Washington, saying, "We are all anxious about the doctor. Not that we have any misgivings as to her ability to pass any reasonable and just examination. But we know that both her sex and her color will be against her."[4]

That concern was laid to rest when Halle completed the exam and did exceptionally well—so well that in the 1892 Medical Association of Alabama (MASA) journal, *Transaction*, special attention was given to her accomplishment. By passing the exam, Halle became the first licensed female physician of any race in the state of Alabama.

In August 1891, Dillon began work at Tuskegee, where her job included establishing a pharmacy on campus and teaching two classes each semester on anatomy and hygiene—and while she was at it, she established a nursing school.

Halle Tanner Dillon remarried in 1894, to the Reverend John Quincy Johnson, and resigned her position at Tuskegee to move to Columbia,

South Carolina, where Johnson became the president of Allen University. Halle and John had three children and moved several times over the years before finally settling in Nashville, where John served as pastor of the St. James AME Church. Halle passed away in Columbia in April 1901 due to complications during childbirth, but she will always be remembered for her three short years at Tuskegee, where she became a role model for women of all races across the country.

1. Martha V. Bouyer, "Beyond the Book: The Life and Legacy of Halle Tanner Dillon Johnson," November 1, 2022, https://alafricanamerican.com/wp-content/uploads/2024/06/2022_Beyond-the-Book-doc_NOV.pdf.
2. "Dr. Halle Tanner Dillon Johnson," U.S. National Library of Medicine, June 6, 2022, https://cfmedicine.nlm.nih.gov.
3. Bouyer, "Beyond the Book."
4. Victoria McAfee, "Dr. Halle Tanner Dillon Johnson: A Ground-Breaking Woman Doctor," https://ministryspark.com/wp-content/uploads/06-Dr.HalleTannerDillonJohnson.pdf.

Chapter 25

HELEN KELLER

One of History's Most Remarkable Women

In 1880, in the rural northwestern Alabama town of Tuscumbia, an extraordinary child was born who would grow up to become, as history has noted, one of the most remarkable women in history: Helen Keller. Helen was born to Arthur H. Keller, a former captain in the Confederate army and the editor of the local newspaper, and Kate Adams Keller. The family's ancestors hailed from Switzerland, and quite coincidentally, one of Helen's relatives was the first teacher of the deaf in Zurich, even authoring a book on the subject.

The young Helen was a healthy baby, but at nineteen months old, she contracted an unknown illness. Many historians believe it was either scarlet fever or meningitis.[1] The illness left her deaf and blind. As Hellen grew, she developed her own means of communication to express herself, but her sign language and way of feeling a person's facial expressions were rudimentary at best and quickly became inadequate. Needless to say, Helen was frustrated that she could not communicate and would have uncontrollable episodes of crying. She became an unruly child and suffered frequent wild, angry tantrums. "After a while," she would later write in her book, *The Story of My Life*, "the need of some means of communication became so urgent that these outbursts occurred daily, sometimes hourly."[2]

Her parents worried that their daughter might never be educated or be able to communicate. She needed a teacher, but if they did find a suitable instructor, who would be willing to relocate to the tiny rural town? Their answer came when they read about a doctor, Dr. Howe, who had developed

The young Helen Keller. *Library of Congress Prints and Photographs Division.*

a method of teaching the deaf and blind. The problem was that he had died years before, and presumably, his research died with him.

When Helen was six, Arthur and Kate took her to Baltimore to meet with a renowned occultist, Dr. Chisolm, who they thought might be able to offer some assistance. He recommended that they visit the famous inventor Dr. Alexander Graham Bell, the inventor of the telephone, who had been working with deaf children in Washington, D.C. Helen made an immediate connection with Bell, who understood her signing. He suggested that the Kellers write to the Perkins Institute in Boston, where Dr. Howe had done his research. Perhaps they could be of assistance. Helen's parents did as Bell suggested, and when they returned to Tuscumbia, they found a letter waiting for them stating that the institute had found a teacher who could help Helen: Anne Mansfield Sullivan.

The introduction of Anne Sullivan into Helen's life and the miracle she was about to perform were spiritual experiences for the young girl, as she later wrote: "Thus I came up out of Egypt and stood before Sinai, and a power divine touched my spirit and gave it sight, so that I beheld many wonders. And from the sacred mountain I heard a voice which said, 'Knowledge is love and light and vision.'"[3]

Sullivan arrived at the Keller home, Ivy Green, on March 3, 1887. She was a recent graduate of Perkins with a strong and determined will, one that would be needed with the unruly Helen. The youngster would hit Anne, kick her—she even knocked out one of Anne's teeth. Eventually, Sullivan gained Helen's trust, and her work began in earnest: teaching Helen how to spell using her fingers touching a person's hand. Helen didn't quite grasp what Anne was trying to teach her at first, but it all became clear when one day, Anne started pumping cool water from the home's well into Helen's hand and repeatedly writing the letters W-A-T-E-R in her hand. After much work, the connection was made. It was, indeed, a miracle. By nightfall, Helen had learned 30 words, and in six months, she had learned 625 words.[4]

When Helen was ten, Anne Sullivan took her to the Perkins Institute, where she learned braille and how to use a specially designed typewriter. She attended the Horace Mann School for the Deaf in Boston, where teacher Sarah Fuller helped her improve her speech. Eventually, she went to the Cambridge School for Young Ladies, and soon after, with Sullivan's help, she was admitted to Radcliffe College, where she graduated cum laude in 1904. Before graduating, she launched her writing career and authored two books, *The Story of My Life* (1902) and *Optimism* (1903).

There was no stopping Helen as she began authoring numerous articles on the prevention of blindness in children and toured the world lecturing as an advocate for the blind. When Anne Sullivan married John Macy in 1905, Helen moved in with the couple, and Macy's interest in politics rubbed off on Helen. She became a pacifist during World War I, and along with her friends Jane Adams and Crystal Eastman, she cofounded the American Civil Liberties Union (ACLU). She also became a leading voice in the suffrage movement, advocating for women's rights.

Anne Sullivan passed away in 1936, and her ashes were interred in the columbarium in Washington's National Cathedral, but her death did not stop Helen. With the help of other aides, she continued to write and lecture, and she toured military hospitals during World War II. A play was written about the life of Anne Sullivan, *The Miracle Worker*, which began its run in 1955 and won two Pulitzer Prizes. The play was turned into a movie starring Patty Duke Astin and Anne Bancroft in 1962 that won two Academy Awards.

Before she died, Helen Keller was nominated for the Nobel Peace Prize in 1954, was awarded the Presidential Medal of Honor in 1964 and met every president from Grover Cleveland to John F. Kennedy (that's twelve in all). Helen passed away on June 1, 1968. Her ashes were interred next to Anne Sullivan's in the National Cathedral, a fitting ending to this story of a true miracle.

---

1. "The Biography of Helen Keller," Ivy Green, February 2, 2022, https://helenkellerbirthplace.org.
2. Helen Keller and John Albert Macy, *The Story of My Life with Her Letters (1887–1901) and a Supplementary Account of Her Education, Including Passages from the Reports and Letters of Her Teacher Anne Mansfield Sullivan* (Doubleday, Page, 1903), 17.
3. Keller and Macy, *Story of My Life*, 20.
4. "Helen Keller Biography," American Foundation for the Blind, https://www.afb.org; "Biography of Helen Keller," Ivy Green.

Chapter 26

MAUD McLURE KELLY

Alabama's First Female Lawyer

Maud McLure was born into a prominent Alabama family and lived a privileged life with a house full of servants, books and all the trappings of opulent living. But that wasn't the life the young woman from Oxford, Alabama, wanted. Instead, she put her intelligence and determination to use and beat the odds during a time when men were virtually running the world, opening a door that thousands of women in the state would soon walk through themselves when she became the first female lawyer in Alabama.

Her father, Richard Bussey Kelly, was a lawyer in Oxford, and after Maud graduated from the Anniston Noble Institute, he moved the family to Birmingham to open a practice. Maud was fascinated with law, so much so that she immersed herself in her father's law books while working as a stenographer in his law firm. She decided to attend law school and applied to sit for the entrance exam for the University of Alabama Law School in 1907. Reading all those law books must have paid off, because she did so well on the exam that she was admitted as a senior—only the second woman ever admitted to the school—and only one year later, she graduated with honors.[1]

Having a stellar academic career is all well and good, but Maud would have to contend with the reality of the time: the law was a male-dominated field, especially in Alabama, where the Code of Alabama specifically stated that "anyone who presented his diploma would be allowed to try a case."[2] Maud's law degree would be of no use unless things changed. And they did. Her friend and classmate John McDuffie introduced a bill in the Alabama legislature to change the wording of the code.[3] The bill passed in November 1907, and Maud was admitted to the Alabama Bar on October 7, 1908—it was, she said, her greatest accomplishment.

Maud opened her own law practice in Birmingham and represented a wide variety of clients and cases, both civil and criminal, becoming an advocate for the poor and underserved in the Birmingham area. She also became a strong voice for women's rights and the suffrage movement as she fought for ratification of the Nineteenth Amendment to the U.S. Constitution. Maud Kelly eventually moved to Washington, D.C., where in 1914 she added to her illustrious legal career by becoming one of the first women from the South to be certified to argue cases before the U.S. Supreme Court. She also became an attorney for the U.S. Department of the Interior.

Besides law, Maud McLure Kelly had a passion for history. After the death of her father in 1924, she returned to Alabama and continued her practice in Birmingham but also became an archivist, traveling across the state with Marie Bankhead Owen to gather historical information on prominent families, state officials, public land records, early government proceedings and more. She later joined the Alabama Department of Archives and History, which was the recipient of all her and Owen's research.

Maud retired from practicing law in 1931 but continued doing historical archiving and volunteering for civic and charitable causes until her death in 1973. In 2002, Maud McLure Kelly was honored by the Alabama State Bar Association when it established the Maud McLure Kelly Award, which is presented each year to a "female attorney who has made a lasting impact on the legal profession and has been a pioneer and leader within the state."

---

1. "Maud McLure Kelly (1887–1973)," Alabama Women's Hall of Fame, http://www.awhf.org.
2. Jennifer Taylor, "Maud McLure Kelly," Samford University Special Collections Treasures, May 2007, https://library.samford.edu.
3. Taylor, "Maud McLure Kelly.

Chapter 27

CORETTA SCOTT KING

The Seasoned Civil Rights Campaigner

"What did it take to stay on the civil rights battlefield after Martin was assassinated?" Coretta Scott King wrote. "I never knew if the same hate that killed my husband would claim my life or the lives of my children.... You never knew the stresses and strains I underwent as a woman in a male-dominated culture, because I didn't complain. I didn't break."[1]

That is how Coretta Scott King, the wife of civil rights icon Martin Luther King Jr., began her autobiography. It was an attempt to explain the trials and tribulations she went through following the death of her husband, but she never complained and never gave up on the dream.

Coretta was born to Obadiah and Bernice Scott near the town of Marion, Alabama, in 1927, the second of three children. Coretta's family was not rich by any means, but they did fairly well for themselves considering the situation for Blacks in the South. Her father was a barber, hauled timber and owned a country store, while her mother was a school bus driver. The children helped out by picking cotton. Coretta's passion in life was music, which she immersed herself in while attending a private missionary institute in Marion. She studied piano and voice, and at fifteen, she became the choir director and pianist of her church's junior choir.

Coretta's early years in school were marred by racial violence. While she was in high school, both her home and her father's sawmill were set on fire.[2] Undaunted, she graduated from Lincoln High School in 1945 as class valedictorian and received a partial scholarship to attend Antioch College in Yellow Springs, Ohio. "The college's emphasis on service to mankind

Dr. Martin Luther King Jr.'s widow, Coretta Scott King, speaks at a 1988 event in which a time capsule holding some of Dr. King's possessions was lowered into the ground at Freedom Plaza on Pennsylvania Avenue, Washington, D.C. *Photographs in the Carol M. Highsmith Archive, Library of Congress, Prints and Photographs Division.*

reinforced the Christian spirit of giving and sharing," she later wrote, and provided "a new self-assurance that encouraged me in competition with all people."[3] While attending Antioch, she became involved politically with groups such as the NAACP and the Race Relations and Civil Liberties Committee. She graduated Antioch with a Bachelor of Arts degree in music and education in 1951 and was awarded a fellowship to continue her studies at the prestigious New England Conservatory of Music (NECM) in Boston. It was here that her life would take a dramatic turn.

In 1952, a friend of both Coretta and Martin Luther King Jr., Mary Powell, thought that they would make the perfect couple. At the time, Martin was working on his doctorate in systematic theology at Boston University. Mary set the couple up on a blind date, and on a cold, wet January evening, Coretta waited patiently outside one of the buildings on the NECM campus for Martin to arrive. Eventually, a green Chevy pulled up. "I waited for him on the steps outside the conservatory on the Huntington Avenue side," she later wrote. "The green car pulled up to the curb, and as I walked down the steps, I could see the young man sitting in the car."

Her first impression was not that this young man would be an iconic civil rights leader but that he looked short and like a boy (he had shaved off his iconic mustache during a fraternity initiation). But within a few minutes of talking with him, she "had completely revised my first impression. He radiated charm. When he talked, he grew in stature. Even when he was so young, he drew people to him from the very first moment with his eloquence, his sincerity, and his moral stature. I knew immediately that he was very special."[4]

It didn't take long before Martin proposed marriage, but Coretta was a little wary of the offer. At the time, she was much more of an activist than Martin, and she worried about how "circumscribed" her life might become if she married a pastor. Eventually, she accepted his proposal, and the couple were married in her hometown on June 18, 1953. The word *obey* was conspicuously missing from their wedding vows. The following year, the Kings moved to Montgomery.

In the years that followed, as Martin became a leader of the Civil Rights Movement, Coretta stood beside him in the fight and continued her own activism. She often put her singing talent to use for the cause, performing in freedom concerts that included lectures, poetry and more; all proceeds from these events were donated to the Southern Christian Leadership Conference.

In December 1955, the Montgomery Bus Boycott began when Rosa Parks refused to give up her seat to a white passenger on a segregated city bus. Martin became the face of the boycott, and his family were the recipients of violent retribution. Their house was firebombed with Coretta and their baby, Yolanda, inside. "I was tested by fire and I came to understand that I was not a breakable crystal figurine," she wrote. "I found I became stronger in a crisis."[5]

The threats continued, including racist phone calls. Coretta would answer the phone and be bombarded with vile, racist death threats. Calmly, she would reply, "My husband is asleep....He told me to write the name and number of anyone who called to threaten his life so that he could return the call and receive the threat in the morning when he wakes up and is fresh."[6]

Throughout the 1960s, Coretta Scott King continued to be a voice for nonviolent solutions to social issues around the world. In 1962, she was a delegate for the Women's Strike for Peace to the seventeen-nation Disarmament Conference in Geneva, Switzerland, and she joined the Women's International League for Peace and Freedom.

On April 4, 1968, Martin Luther King Jr. was assassinated in Memphis, Tennessee. After the tragic death of a loved one, many people might have found themselves stopped in their tracks and paused life while they grieved, but not Coretta. Four days after his death, without missing a beat, she continued her husband's work, leading a protest march that was supposed to have been led by her husband to stand in solidarity with striking sanitation workers in Memphis. Coretta went on to protest the Vietnam War and apartheid in South Africa. She also founded the King Center, which was built next-door to the church where her husband was once the pastor, Ebenezer Baptist in Atlanta. She also lobbied for fifteen years to make Martin's birthday a national holiday. The bill was passed by Congress and signed into law by President Reagan in 1983.

Coretta Scott King passed away in 2006. Her funeral was held at the New Birth Missionary Baptist Church in Stonecrest, Georgia. The service lasted eight hours, and fourteen thousand people attended, including both Presidents Bush, Presidents Clinton and Carter and a future president, Senator Barack Obama.

Coretta's husband, Martin, was once asked by a reporter if he had educated his wife about social justice and made her the successful activist she was. He simply replied, "She educated me."

---

1. Coretta Scott King, *Coretta: My Life, My Love, My Legacy* (Picador, Henry Holt, 2017), 4–5.
2. Jeanne Theoharis, "'I Am Not a Symbol, I Am an Activist': The Untold Story of Coretta Scott King," *Guardian*, February 3, 2018, https://www.theguardian.com.
3. Coretta Scott King, *My Life with Martin Luther King, Jr.* (Hodder & Stoughton, 1970), 43.
4. "Coretta Scott King (1927–2006)," Remember Them, May 7, 2024, https://remember-them.org.
5. Theoharis, "Not a Symbol."
6. Theoharis, "Not a Symbol."

Chapter 28

LILLY LEDBETTER

Grit and Sacrifice for American Women

Imagine that one day, you check your mailbox and find an anonymous note. You open it, and inside, it tells you there is evidence that you are being discriminated against in your workplace because you are a woman—specifically that you are being paid much less than your male counterparts who do the same job. What would you do? For Lilly Ledbetter, the answer was simple: fight back. In doing so, she helped win a major battle for all women in America.

Lilly Lynn McDaniel grew up on a small farm in the rural town of Possum Trot, Alabama. In her youth, she observed the success of a family friend who was able to financially provide for his family and who attributed his prosperity to his job at the Goodyear Tire and Rubber factory in nearby Gadsden. Lilly thought that one day, she would have a job at the plant and be successful, too.

Lilly excelled in high school, but the family could not afford to send her to college. Instead, she married her childhood sweetheart, Charles Ledbetter, not necessarily for love but for a little financial stability. Both Charles and Lilly worked at a General Electric factory, but the company was facing hard times, and the factory closed. Fortunately for Lilly, as the factory closed, an ad appeared in the local newspaper: the Goodyear plant was hiring women to be managers. This was the moment she had been waiting for, and in 1979, at the age of forty-one, she was hired as a full-time manager.[1]

Over the next nineteen years, Lilly was an exceptional employee, winning several achievement and performance awards along the way, but her male

Lilly Ledbetter (*far right*), a women's rights activist whose ten-year battle against her former employer inspired federal law, watches as President Barack Obama signs the Lilly Ledbetter Fair Pay Act in January 2009. *Courtesy Asset/Defense Contract Management Agency.*

colleagues made working at the plant difficult. She was relocated to different departments time and time again. Men made sexual comments to her and made sexual advances, including one of her supervisors, who, when she declined his advances, retaliated by reporting that she was underperforming and was turning in inadequate production numbers.[2]

With the backing of her husband, Lilly filed a complaint with the Equal Employment Opportunity Commission (EEOC) and won the right to sue Goodyear. But Lilly wanted only to be recognized for her work and earn the same amount as her colleagues. She took the high road and decided to settle with the company by accepting a supervisory position they offered her. The title placed her higher up in the chain of command at the plant, and she became her previous supervisor's boss—the same person who had made those advances. But things only got worse for Lilly as rumors began to fly that because of her lawsuit, workers might lose their jobs, inflaming their hatred toward her even more. When notices of pay raises went out to employees, they were usually on official company stationery from human resources. Lilly would receive her notices handwritten on scrap pieces of paper. She was also denied a raise on several occasions. The reason given was that it was due to a "poor performance review," even though she had just won the company's top performance award.

The matter finally boiled over when Lilly received an anonymous note in her mailbox two years before her retirement telling her that her male counterparts were being paid $55,000 a year. Lilly was making only $44,000 for doing the same job.[3] Once again, with the backing of her husband, Lilly filed a formal lawsuit under Title 7 of the Civil Rights Act of 1964. The case went to trial, and the jury found Goodyear guilty and ordered the company to compensate Lilly to the tune of $3.8 million.[4] Goodyear appealed, and the Eleventh Circuit Court of Appeals reversed the lower court decision. Lilly appealed the case to the U.S. Supreme Court. In 2007, in a 5–4 decision, the Supreme Court ruled that employers could not be sued under the act if the claim had been filed outside of a 180-day timeframe and sided with the appeals court ruling. Lilly's claim fell outside of the timeframe, and Lilly and Charles never saw a dime from the action.

Shortly after Lilly Ledbetter retired, she became a champion for equal pay for women and worked tirelessly to make it happen. On January 22, 2009, the U.S. House and Senate passed the Lilly Ledbetter Fair Pay Act and sent it to the White House. It was the first bill signed into law by newly elected president Barack Obama. When Lilly passed away in 2024, President Obama said of her, "Lilly Ledbetter never set out to be a trailblazer or a household name. She just wanted to be paid the same as a man for her hard work. But this grandmother from Alabama kept on fighting until the day I signed the Lilly Ledbetter Fair Pay Act into law."[5]

---

1. Lilly Ledbetter, *Grace and Grit: My Fight for Equal Pay and Fairness at Goodyear and Beyond* (Random House, 2012), 28.
2. Ledbetter, *Grace and Grit*, 91.
3. Ledbetter, *Grace and Grit*, 15.
4. Betsey Danforth, "Driving Miss Lilly: Grace and Grit, Indeed!" Womanifesto (April/May 2014), Montana State University Women's Center, https://www.montana.edu/women/documents/AprilMay2014.pdf.
5. William Thornton, "Obama Pays Tribute to Lilly Ledbetter: This Grandmother from Alabama Kept on Fighting," AL.com, October 13, 2024, https://www.al.com.

Chapter 29

HARPER LEE

American Novelist, Alabama Treasure

The quaint Alabama town of Monroeville was once known as a crossroads community. Located just south of the state's plantation region, the Black Belt, and the state's Port City on the Gulf Coast, Mobile, the town was once a thriving agricultural community and then, later, a major textile manufacturing town. But in the 1950s, Monroeville became something more. Its moniker became the Literary Capital of Alabama, and it was because of one woman: Nell Harper Lee.

The daughter of Amasa Coleman and Francis Cunningham Finch Lee, young Harper was a ferocious reader and a tomboy. One of her best friends and neighbors growing up in Monroeville was future award-winning author Truman Capote; their friendship would catapult both writers to literary stardom.

Two events in Harper's early life played a pivotal role in her future writing. The first dealt with her father, Amasa. Amasa was the editor of the local paper, a business owner, a state legislator and a county lawyer. As a lawyer, in 1931, Amasa defended two Black men accused of murdering a white storekeeper, an event that would later find its way into Harper's writing. The two men were found guilty by the jury and sentenced to death.

The other event occurred in April 1931, when the trial of nine young Black men accused of raping two white women began. Before the jury was even seated, the accused barely escaped a lynching, and no lawyer would represent them until one finally accepted the case the day before the trial began. Although one of the accusers recanted her initial testimony during the trial and evidence from the initial medical examination of the woman refuted the rape charge, it didn't matter. The all-white jury convicted the accused, and eight of the nine were sentenced to death. The ninth was twelve years old at the time. After six years of appeals, all but one of the nine men were either freed or paroled.[1] News of the trial left a deep impression on Harper. She used her father as the model for her immortal character Atticus Finch, and the rape trial became the basis for her famous novel *To Kill a Mockingbird*.

For a time, Harper thought about following in her father's footsteps, and she enrolled at the University of Alabama School of Law in 1945. After spending a year studying at Oxford University, she realized that law wasn't for her, and when she returned to the United States, she dropped out of college to immerse herself in her writing. At the age of twenty-three, Harper took an apartment in New York City and worked as a ticketing agent for British Overseas Airlines. She found it difficult to make ends meet in the big city, but as luck would have it, she made friends with Broadway composer and lyricist Michael Martin Brown and his wife, Joy. They became close friends, and in 1956, the couple presented Harper with an extraordinary Christmas present: they supported Harper financially for one year so she could focus on her writing. They also found her a literary agent, Maurice Crain.[2]

While in New York, Harper Lee met up with her friend Truman Capote and became his research assistant for a project he was working on, an article for *The New Yorker* about the murder of a family on a small Kansas farm. Eventually, that article would be transformed into Capote's own best-selling book *In Cold Blood*, with which Harper Lee assisted in preparing the galley copies.[3]

It took Harper two years to complete the work on her novel *To Kill a Mockingbird*. Her agent immediately sent it off for consideration to Lippincott Publishing, and it was published in 1960. The book was a tremendous hit, so much so that its sales were described as a "summer storm."[4] One year after its release, it had sold over 500,000 copies—not bad for a small first printing of 5,000 copies. By the end of 1961, it had sold over 15 million copies and won the Pulitzer Prize. Soon, it became required reading in many schools across the country. That same year, the book was made into a movie starring Gregory Peck, which won two Academy Awards.

When Peck was asked about what it was like working with Harper Lee on the movie, he recalled one moment when he was filming a scene in which Atticus Finch was walking home and was greeted by his children. Peck saw

Harper off to the side watching them film the scene and thought he saw tears in her eyes. "I thought, *We're just tearing her up*," he told an audience during an interview with the American Film Institute. "*We're breaking her up. We must be marvelous*....So I walked over and said, 'Harper, I think I saw some tears on your cheeks.'...She said, 'Oh, Gregory, you've got a little potbelly just like my daddy.'"[5]

The awards and accolades for her book continued until her death in 2016. She was named to the National Council of the Arts by President Lyndon B. Johnson in 1966 and was awarded the National Medal of Arts by President Obama in 2010.

On February 3, 2015, the publishing company Harper Collins announced that a second book by Harper Lee would be released, titled *Go Set a Watchman*. Many thought it would be a completely new novel, but in fact, it was basically a rough draft of *Mockingbird*. It didn't matter. The book was an overnight success, selling 720,000 copies within thirty-six hours.[6] By the time of her death, *Mockingbird* had sold over 50 million copies.

Harper Lee passed away on February 19, 2016, at her home in Monroeville. The town commemorates the author's life and *To Kill a Mockingbird* annually with a weekend of lectures, readings and a live production of the play outside of the book's centerpiece, the old county courthouse itself.[7]

---

1. "A Short Biography of Harper Lee," Grade Saver, https://www.gradesaver.com.
2. "Harper Lee," Biography, March 31, 2021, https://www.biography.com.
3. "Harper Lee," Biography.
4. "Harper Lee," Encyclopedia of Alabama, February 5, 2024, https://encyclopediaofalabama.org.
5. American Film Institute, "Gregory Peck Tells a Story About Harper Lee While Filming *To Kill a Mockingbird*," YouTube, April 5, 2020, https://youtu.be/Q0ZILl2Om5A.
6. "Harper Lee," Encyclopedia of Alabama.
7. "To Kill a Mockingbird," Mockingbird Company, https://www.tokillamockingbird.com/the-play.

Chapter 30

OCTAVIA WALTON LE VERT

The Pride of Mobile

Just north of the Gulf of Mexico, along the banks of the wide bay that bears its name, the city of Mobile has seen its share of history. The settlement that would become the state's Port City was first occupied by Europeans—the French—in 1702. Following the War of 1812 and up until the Civil War, during the antebellum period, the city experienced phenomenal growth as a seaport with shipbuilding and trade making it one of the most unique and prosperous cities along the Gulf Coast. It is during this time that we find our next story about an extraordinary Alabama woman, one of the city's most celebrated of the time: Octavia Walton Le Vert.

Octavia came from a prominent Georgia family. She was the granddaughter of George Walton, who fought in the American Revolution and was a member of the Second Congressional Congress, one of the signers of the Declaration of Independence and a senator from Georgia.

Born on August 11, 1811, Octavia Celestia Valentine Walton did not have a formal education but instead was taught by her highly educated mother, Sarah Minge Walker Walton, her grandmother and a Scottish tutor. By the age of twelve, she had already learned six languages and could play music and paint—plus, her family's social standing allowed her to hobnob with many notable luminaries of the day. As author Paula Webb commented in her biography of Octavia, the young woman had a unique curiosity about the world and people around her. All who knew her described the young woman as being captivating, having a strong intellect and a kind heart.[1]

Between 1812 and 1821, Octavia's father, a prominent lawyer, was a member of the Georgia state legislature. In 1821, when Octavia was twelve

Madame Octavia Le Vert. *Mobile Public Library Local History & Genealogy.*

years old, her father was appointed Florida's first territorial secretary, and the family moved to Pensacola. The territory had recently been ceded to the United States by Spain (another country that once controlled the region), and as such, there were many documents and letters written in both French and Spanish. Octavia assisted her father in translating these documents.

In 1835, the family moved to Mobile, where Octavia would begin her reign over that city's elite society. Her father opened a law office on Government Street, which still stands today. One year after moving to Mobile, Octavia married Henry Strachey LeVert, a prominent physician. She was a very independent woman for her time. Henry spelled his last name as one word, but Octavia insisted on using the original French spelling, Le Vert, and asked to be addressed as Madame, not Mrs.[2]

Octavia became the most widely known socialite not only on the Gulf Coast but in the country. During this time, Mobile was captivated by wealth, prestige and status. If you were lower down in the societal hierarchy and wanted your status elevated in the city, simply being seen in the company of Octavia or receiving an invitation to her home would do the trick. Octavia entertained frequently, keeping her home open to receive guests practically every day from eleven o'clock in the morning to eleven o'clock in the evening.[3] And on any given night, you never knew who might be in attendance: famous writers, politicians and dignitaries such as Edgar Allan Poe, Daniel Webster and, most notably, writer Washington Irving, who became a close friend of the socialite and encouraged her to author a book. Irving wrote that Octavia was "a woman such as appears but once in the course of an empire."[4]

Octavia traveled the world and visited Europe, many times escorted by President Millard Filmore, where she met with the Pope, Queen Victoria, Prince Albert and Napolean. But while touring those countries, she also saw firsthand the poverty that gripped much of the continent, and she related stories about the plight of those who were suffering to women back home in the States, telling them about women who were forced to work in sweatshops or pick cotton and hoe fields on struggling farms and about the general welfare of the women she saw who were trying to make it in a man's world.

When she returned to the States, Octavia became a charter member of the Sorosis Club, an organization founded during Reconstruction following the Civil War to improve women's education, unite women for mutual assistance and represent women in art, literature and science. In 1855, Octavia Le Vert was appointed Alabama's commissioner to the Paris Exposition by Governor John A. Winston. The exposition gave cities and countries from around the world the chance to showcase their art, culture and industry to millions of visitors. Octavia would be the only female commissioner at the expo. The position was more of an honorary one than anything else, due to the fact that the state did not send her with any displays or literature to showcase products made in Alabama. When someone would ask her to show them something that came from her state, she could only point to her daughter.[5]

Just prior to the outbreak of the Civil War, Octavia completed a book, a two-volume set called *Souvenirs of Travel*, which described her adventures traveling the world. But soon after, the drumbeat of war could be heard; the South's secession from the Union was on the horizon. Octavia was not in favor of secession, and her leanings toward the Union following the war would be her downfall.

When she heard the news that General Lee had surrendered to General Grant at Appomattox Court House in Virginia, Octavia rushed over to the home of Confederate navy Admiral Raphael Semmes, who also resided in Mobile, and cheered the Union victory. Legend has it that the admiral's daughter threw Octavia out of their house.[6] When the Union army finally captured Mobile, the last remaining Confederate port city, Octavia befriended many Yankee soldiers and went as far as to entertain Yankee officers in her home. The "Pride of Mobile" was now shunned by fellow Mobilians. After her husband passed away in 1864, her wealth slowly trickled away, and she moved to Augusta, Georgia, where she died in 1877.

---

1. Paula Lenor Webb, *Such a Woman: The Life of Madame Octavia Le Vert* (Intellect Publishing, 2021), 90.
2. Sally Pearsall Ericson, "A Famous Mobilian You Should Know: Octavia Walton Le Vert, the Ultimate Southern Belle," AL.com, November 1, 2013, https://www.al.com.

3. Russell Blount, "Madame Octavia LeVert's Salon of the South: The Rise and Fall of a Mobile Icon," *Mobile Bay Magazine*, November 16, 2022, https://mobilebaymag.com.
4. Blount, "Salon of the South."
5. "Octavia Walton Le Vert," Encyclopedia of Alabama, https://encyclopediaofalabama.org.
6. Ericson, "Octavia Walton Le Vert."

Chapter 31

VIVIAN MALONE

Defying Discrimination

It was an event that was broadcast around the world. Alabama Governor George C. Wallace stood on the steps of Foster Auditorium on the campus of the University of Alabama and read from a prepared speech refusing to allow two Black students to enroll in the college. Wallace's defiant act became known as the infamous "Stand in the Schoolhouse Door." One of the two students attempting to enroll was twenty-year-old Vivian Malone.

The Mobile native was born in 1942. Both her parents had good jobs working at Brookley Field, a major Army Air Force supply base in Mobile, and were involved in the Civil Rights Movement. Vivian was an exceptional student, graduating in 1960 from Central High School in Mobile, where she was a member of the National Honor Society. During her public school years, Vivian was involved in a number of community organizations that were working to end racial discrimination and promote school desegregation.

Following graduation, Vivian earned a two-year degree in business education from Alabama A&M University. Unfortunately, the college lost its accreditation, so to receive an accredited degree, Vivian and two hundred other Black students applied for admission to the University of Alabama's Mobile campus. All the applications were denied either because "enrollment had closed" or the school was "over enrollment." The truth of the matter was that Alabama's segregation laws prohibited their admission.[1] Undaunted, Vivian and another Black student, James Hood, filed a lawsuit through

Vivian Malone, one of the first African Americans to attend the University of Alabama and the first to graduate, walks through a crowd that includes photographers, National Guard members and Deputy U.S. Attorney General Nicholas Katzenbach, 1963. *Leffler, Warren K, photographer. Library of Congress.*

the Legal Defense Fund (LDF) for admission to the university's School of Commerce and Business Administration. The legal battle took one year, and in the end, U.S. District Court Judge Harlan Grooms ordered the college to open its doors to the students.

On June 11, 1963, a three-car motorcade pulled up to the campus's Foster Auditorium. Inside the car rode U.S. Deputy Attorney General Nicholas Katzenbach, a small army of federal marshals, Vivian Malone and James Hood. The event was quite the spectacle: the press and hundreds of onlookers lined the walkway leading to the building. Katzenbach introduced himself to Wallace, who was waiting at the entrance, and made it perfectly clear what his intentions were. So did Wallace. Reading a prepared script from a podium, with a group of Alabama state troopers behind him blocking the doorway, Wallace proclaimed,

> *I deem it to be my solemn obligation and duty to stand before you representing the rights and sovereignty of this State and its peoples....Being mindful of my duties and responsibilities under the Constitution of the United States, the Constitution of the State of Alabama, and seeking to preserve and maintain the peace and dignity of this State, and the individual freedoms*

> *of the citizens thereof, [I] do hereby denounce and forbid this illegal and unwarranted action by the Central Government.*[2]

Katzenbach politely listened to the speech with an almost "You know where this is heading, don't you?" attitude and then replied, "Governor, I'm not interested in show. I don't know what the purpose of the show is. I am interested in the orders of this court being enforced."[3] President John F. Kennedy was one step ahead of the governor: prior to the motorcade's arrival, he had ordered the federalization of the state's National Guard, effectively stripping Wallace of his command powers. Almost five hours later, one hundred guardsmen escorted the students into the college to complete registration—surprisingly, to cheers and applause of support from many white students who watched the procession. Once inside, Vivian was accepted as a junior.

Vivian and James were not the first Black students to enroll at the college. That honor, as it were, went to Autherine Lucy, who enrolled at the school in 1956 to pursue a master's degree in library science. Only three days into her first semester, the threats to her life were too much. Autherine was suspended and then expelled from the university—as they put it, "for her own safety."

Although Vivian and James were greeted by some of the white students, more often than not, they were subjected to incredibly vile and racist comments and threats. In November 1963, three bombs rocked the campus, one of them only four blocks from Vivian's dormitory. The threats were, understandably, too much for James, who left the university after two months wanting to "avoid a complete mental and physical breakdown."[4] Vivian, on the other hand, stood her ground. The day after her enrollment in the college, civil rights activist Medgar Evans was killed. In a 2004 interview with the *Syracuse Post Standard*, she said, "I decided not to show any fear and went to classes that day."[5] And she did, eventually becoming the first Black student to graduate from the University of Alabama in 1965, with a degree in business management. While she was at the college, the university made the decision to hire a driver to transport her around campus and keep her safe. His name was Mack Jones, and before long, the two fell in love and after her graduation, they married.

The couple moved to Washington, D.C., where Vivian began work with the civil rights division of the U.S. Justice Department. She also worked several years with the Environmental Protection Agency as director of civil rights and urban affairs and director of environmental justice before retiring in 1996. That same year, former Governor Wallace established the Lurleen

B. Wallace Award for Courage. The award was named in honor of his wife and bestowed upon persons who had made significant contributions to the advancement of women. Wallace presented the first award to Vivian Malone Jones. After the presentation, Wallace met with Vivian and admitted that he had made a mistake thirty-three years prior. "I asked him why did he do it," she said. "He said he did what he felt needed to be done at that point in time, but he would not do that today. At that point, we spoke—I spoke—of forgiveness."[6]

In 2000, Vivian was asked to give the commencement address for graduates of the University of Alabama. In her remarks, she urged the graduates to push open closed doors they might encounter.

> *You may not live in a time of great social change as I did, but you will just as certainly face moral choices. There will come a day in your life when you must act for others—your family, perhaps your community—and you must be ready. What you have done to reach this milestone today is part of that preparation. So take from all the books you have read, all the lessons you have learned, the certain knowledge that one day, any day, you must be bold, have courage, and walk through a door that leads to opportunity for others.*[7]

Vivian Malone Jones passed away in 2005. In 2021, she was inducted into Alabama Female Firsts at Stillman College, a program that recognizes women in Alabama who have achieved significant milestones in their careers and leadership. That same year, she was inducted into the Alabama Women's Hall of Fame.

---

1. "Scholarship Recipients: Vivian Malone Jones," Legal Defense Fund, July 7, 2018, https://www.naacpldf.org.
2. "Schoolhouse Door Speech," Emerson Kent, https://www.emersonkent.com.
3. theGrio, "A Confrontation for Integration at the University of Alabama," YouTube, February 26, 2013, https://youtu.be/4WbLGlIzW88.
4. Douglas Martin, "Vivian Malone Jones, 63, Dies; First Black Graduate of University of Alabama," *New York Times*, October 14, 2005.
5. Martin, "Vivian Malone Jones."
6. Phillip Rawls, "Vivian Malone (Jones) (1942–2005)," Associated Press, October 13, 2005, https://www.crmvet.org/mem/malonev.htm.
7. "Vivian Malone Jones (1942–2005)," Alabama Women's Hall of Fame, http://www.awhf.org.

Chapter 32

FRAN McKEE

Advancing Women's Roles in the Navy

The United States Navy was first established as an all-male branch of the military by Congress in 1775. It was not until the United States entered World War I that the secretary of the navy, Josephus Daniels, authorized women to enlist, not in the regular navy but in a volunteer reserve force. The first woman to enlist was Loretta Walsh, who signed up on March 21, 1917. It would take another twenty-five years for women to be allowed to become officers. On July 30, 1942, President Roosevelt signed Public Law 689, which established the Women Accepted for Volunteer Emergency Service (WAVES), a navy reserve program. The former president of Massachusetts' Wellesley College, Mildred McAfee, was sworn in as the navy's first female line officer only two weeks later and was assigned to be the first director of the WAVES.

From then on, women were allowed to enter the navy as line officers, but rising to the rank of flag officer proved difficult. The rule restricting women from being promoted to the highest ranks in the service was changed by Congress in 1967, but it would still take another nine years before the barrier was officially broken by Florence, Alabama native Fran McKee. Fran was the oldest of three daughters born to Thomas Walker and Geneva Lumpkins McKee. Her father was a special investigator for Southern Railroad, a job that forced his family to relocate many times during Fran's young life. Fran was a bright, intelligent young woman who excelled in public school, graduating from Phillips High School in Birmingham at the age of fifteen.[1]

Following public school, Fran went on to earn a Bachelor of Science degree in chemistry from the University of Alabama, and in 1950, she was commissioned as an ensign in the navy. During this time, she continued her education: she earned a master's in international affairs from George Washington University and was awarded a doctorate in public administration from the Massachusetts Maritime Academy. But that was only the beginning for Fran, who became one of the first two women to attend and graduate from the Naval War College, and on June 1, 1976, she became the first woman line officer to attain flag rank in U.S. Naval history when she was promoted to lower half (one star) rear admiral. Two years later, she was fully promoted to upper half (two star) rear admiral.

During her career, Fran McKee served in administrative positions in Morocco and San Francisco as part of the Chief of Naval Reserve Training staff, was the officer in charge of the Naval Women's Officer School in Rhode Island and served as personnel officer at Naval Station Rota (Spain). She also became the first woman to command a naval security group.[2]

Prior to her retirement in 1981, Fran was a champion for women's rights in the military, serving as the senior female officer on the Committee to Study Equal Rights for Women, whose work resulted in sweeping changes in navy policy for female members.[3]

Rear Admiral Fran McKee passed away in 2002 and was buried in Arlington National Cemetery with full honors. As author Parmis Hekhamenesh wrote of the admiral for *Alabama Heritage* magazine, "The contributions and example [set by Fran McKee] paved the way for women in the Navy."[4]

---

1. "Fran McKee (1926–2002)," Alabama Women's Hall of Fame, http://www.awhf.org.
2. "Fran McKee: Rear Admiral," U.S. Navy, https://www.navy.mil.
3. "Fran McKee," Alabama Women's Hall of Fame.
4. Parmis Hekhamenesh, "Admiral Fran McKee: Advancing Women's Roles in the U.S. Navy and Gender Equality," Alabama Heritage, May 8, 2024, https://www.alabamaheritage.com.

Chapter 33

JULIETTE HAMPTON MORGAN

Librarian and Racial Justice Activist

We often picture librarians as quiet bastions of knowledge, our go-to when we need some little piece of obscure information. Even in this day and age, when Google has virtually taken over this role, we still rely on librarians and library researchers to help us dig deeper into history, literature and science. But a librarian as an activist in the fight to end segregation in the South? That was the mission Juliette Hampton Morgan set for herself.

Juliette was a Montgomery native born into a family with deep Southern roots. Her mother, Lila Bess Olin, was a descendant of Confederate General and South Carolina Governor Wade Hampton. She was described by friends and family as a true Southern belle.[1] Her father, Frank Perryman Morgan, was the grandson of a Georgia state legislator. He would later have political aspirations of his own, becoming the first mayor of Heflin, Alabama, and then making a run for Alabama governor but losing the election.

Born in 1914, Juliette glided through high school, graduating from Sidney Lanier in Montgomery in 1930 before heading off to the University of Alabama, where she earned bachelor's and master's degrees in English. When she returned to Montgomery, she began teaching at her alma mater, Sidney Lanier High School, until she was offered a position as assistant librarian in 1942 at the city's Carnegie library. Ten years later, she was promoted to research superintendent of the Montgomery County Public Library. It was at this time that her activism began in earnest as she joined a local Democratic club and wrote countless letters to newspapers and legislators in support of anti-lynching laws and abolishing the poll tax that prevented many Blacks from voting. She also volunteered with activist groups, including the Fellowship of the Concerned and the Alabama Council on Human Relations.[2]

Juliette suffered from severe anxiety and had frequent panic attacks that prevented her from driving a car, so she had no choice but to use public transportation. Throughout the 1950s, the Montgomery bus system had a segregation policy that required Black passengers to step onto the bus through the front door, pay their fare, exit the bus and then climb back onto the bus through the back door and take a seat in the back of the bus.

Juliette was outraged when she saw firsthand the attitudes and actions of the bus drivers toward Black passengers. For example, when a Black passenger would pay their fare, instead of handing them their change, the driver would throw it on the floor. Some drivers would drive past bus stops where Black passengers were waiting, especially when it was cold and rainy. "I have heard some bus drivers use the tone and manners of mule drivers in their treatment of Negro passengers," she once wrote.[3]

Long before the Montgomery Bus Boycott began, Juliette witnessed one incident that finally set her off and demanded action. While she was riding a city bus one evening, the driver made a stop and allowed a Black woman to enter and pay her fare. The woman exited the bus and then went to enter through the rear entrance. As she stepped off the bus, the driver slammed the door and drove away. Juliette jumped from her seat and pulled the emergency cord, alerting the driver to stop the bus. She approached the driver and demanded he let the woman on.

From that moment on, Juliette would disrupt any and all bus service anytime she saw abuses against Black passengers. In 1952, she began writing letters to the local newspaper, the *Montgomery Advertiser*, warning that the bus segregation law had to be changed or there would be consequences. The letter sparked outrage throughout the city. Many of her longtime friends, former students and even family members shunned her. Montgomery Mayor William A. Gayle urged the library board to fire her, but they refused. She did, however, have to promise not to write any more inflammatory letters to the editor.[4]

Juliette stayed true to her word until Autherine Lucy enrolled at the University of Alabama in Tuscaloosa, Juliette's alma mater—the first Black student to do so. Even though Autherine was expelled shortly after enrolling "for her own safety," as university officials put it, it didn't quell the racist violence that broke out across Tuscaloosa. The editor of the *Tuscaloosa News*, Buford Boone, urged the White Citizen's Council in the city to end the violence. In response, Juliette wrote a letter to Boone congratulating him for taking a stand.

When the Montgomery Bus Boycott began in 1955, Juliette wrote to the *Montgomery Advertiser* once again, equating the protestors with Gandhi. "The Negroes of Montgomery," she wrote, "seem to have taken a lesson from Gandhi....Their own task is greater than Gandhi's however, for they have greater prejudice to overcome."[5] That was the last straw for Mayor Gayle, who once again demanded Juliette be fired. And once again, the library board refused. White library patrons tore up their cards and boycotted the Montgomery library system in protest.

On June 15, 1957, a cross was set on fire on the front lawn of Juliette's apartment building. Under unsurmountable pressure, Juliette Hampton Morgan relented and voluntarily resigned her position with the library system. The following day, she was found dead in her home from an overdose of sleeping pills. Her funeral was attended by many, both Black and white. Many of the white attendees included those who had previously shunned Juliette or attacked her for her views and felt remorse over her death.

It would take another five years for the Montgomery public library system to be integrated. In 2005, the central branch of the library was named in Juliette's honor. That same year, she was inducted into the Alabama Women's Hall of Fame. For her extraordinary efforts in the fight for civil rights, Martin Luther King Jr. vowed that her name would be remembered by future generations.[6]

---

1. "Juliette Hampton Morgan," Encyclopedia of Alabama, June 30, 2008, https://encyclopediaofalabama.org.
2. "Juliette Hampton Morgan," Encyclopedia of Alabama.
3. "Juliette Hampton Morgan, Librarian and Civil Rights Activist," Alabama Department of Archives & History, YouTube, June 5, 2020, 1:11 to 1:14, https://youtu.be/yVDLdyoWCVg.
4. "Juliette Hampton Morgan," Encyclopedia of Alabama.
5. Jeff Sapp, *Juliette Hampton Morgan: A White Woman Who Understood* (Civil Rights Memorial Center, 2006), 8.
6. Mary Stanton, *Journey Toward Justice: Juliette Hampton Morgan and the Montgomery Bus Boycott* (University of Georgia Press, 2006), ix.

Chapter 34

SISTER CHRYSOSTOM MOYNAHAN

A Call to Service

Up until 1633, Catholic nuns led a cloistered life, giving up worldly goods and possessions, living in a nunnery and leading a life of contemplation and prayer. In 1633, that began to change as Sisters became more active in society, helping the poor and needy and tending to the sick. In that year, St. Vincent de Paul and St. Louise de Marillac Churches formed the Daughters of Charity in Paris, France. The order would consist of a group of young women who shared a deep dedication to and passion for aiding the sick and poor. The Daughters opened soup kitchens, established schools and homes for orphans and organized hospitals.[1]

Hannah Moynahan was born in Ireland and immigrated with her parents to Massachusetts in 1879. After graduating from the Daughters of Charity seminary in 1889, she was dispatched for service to Carney Hospital in Boston and attended its school for nurses, graduating in 1894. In 1900, she came to Alabama, where she became the administrator of St. Vincent's Hospital in Birmingham. Her job responsibilities included supervising nursing care, organizing the medical staff and its residency program, managing finances and developing programs that would provide hospital services to those who could not pay. She also organized the Ladies Charity of Birmingham to assist poor families financially.

During her eighteen years at the hospital, in between all the other work she had signed on for, Sister Moynahan worked diligently to obtain her nursing license, which she did on March 10, 1916. Her license number was 1—as she was the first registered nurse in Alabama. Sister Moynahan's call to service would expand dramatically in 1918 when, along with nine other Daughters of Charity, she was called on to aid the sick and wounded on the Western

Front during World War I. The group hospital they manned was to be called Base Hospital 102, but so many of the women who were sent over were from New Orleans' Loyola University that the unit became unofficially known as the Loyola Unit.[2] Sister Moynahan was appointed the hospital's chief nurse.[3]

Just prior to departing Baltimore for Europe, Sister Moynahan was asked by a reporter with the *El Paso Herald* about being sent to the front.

> *We are all registered nurses and are anxious to go across and get to work.... We will have charge of the operating rooms and hope to do our full duty to bring the American boys back to health and happiness.... The sisterhood feels keenly the desire to be of the utmost service in caring for the soldiers of Italy or any of the other Allies of America. War makes its demand upon the woman power of America as well as upon the man power, and all who can do so, no matter what the sacrifice, should serve the interest of America's part in the war.*[4]

On the way to Europe, the ship they sailed on, the *Umbria*, stopped to rescue survivors of the oil tanker *Jennings*, which had been sunk by Germany's *U-140* submarine one hundred miles off the coast of Virginia. When the women arrived at their destination, the base hospital was established in Vicenza, Italy, an area fifteen miles away from the front that had been declared a war zone three years earlier. Besides the medical staff, the Sisters supervised a staff of ninety nurses and five professional staff nurses at the one-thousand-bed hospital, all of whom were inducted into the U.S. Army Nurse Corps Reserve for their one year of service. In that year and under the Sisters' care, over three thousand U.S., Italian, French, British and Czech soldiers were treated for exposure to mustard gas, malaria and influenza. Of those, only twenty-eight died.

On her return to America in 1919, Sister Moynahan was decorated by both the U.S. and Italian governments for her bravery and service during the war. She returned to become administrator of hospitals in St. Louis, Missouri, before returning to Alabama to become the administrator of Providence Hospital in Mobile, where she continued her work until her death in 1941. Sister Moynahan led a full life, heeding the call to service and never once shying away from that calling.

---

1. "Who We Are," Daughters of Charity, May 18, 2012, https://daughtersofcharity.org.

2. Elizabeth Foxwell, "Sister Chrysostom Moynahan: AEF Chief Nurse Buried with Military Honors," *American Women in World War I* (blog), November 11, 2017, https://americanwomeninwwi.wordpress.com.
3. Foxwell, "Sister Chrysostom Moynahan."
4. "A Part of Loyola Unit of One Hundred Sisters," *El Paso Herald*, April 24, 1918, https://chroniclingamerica.loc.gov.

Chapter 35

ODETTA

The Voice of the Civil Rights Movement

We are far enough removed from the civil unrest of the 1950s and '60s that some people believe the South's strict Jim Crow laws of segregation and discrimination against Black Americans did not infiltrate the music industry. Today, we can plug a CD into a player, put the tone arm on a vinyl disc or turn on SiriusXM and hear phenomenal music by the great Black artists of that era. It's almost as if their journey to stardom was an easy ride. But as with all other aspects of life in the mid-twentieth century, even recording studios were segregated, a situation that confronted one of America's great folk singers and a voice that would power the Civil Rights Movement: Odetta Holmes, better known simply as Odetta.

Odetta Holmes was born in Birmingham in the middle of the Great Depression and, as a child, saw firsthand the disparity between whites and Blacks—the segregated water fountains, movie theaters and restaurants. She recalled that her first direct run-in with racism came in 1937, when her family was moving to Los Angeles. When they boarded the train, the conductor yelled racial slurs at them and forcibly pushed them to a car labeled "Coloreds Only."[1] This and similar incidents angered Odetta, a feeling that she needed to express—but how?

After her father passed away when Odetta was very young, her mother, Flora, packed up her two daughters and moved to Los Angeles. From an early age, Odetta loved music, and she and her sister Jimmie Lee would spend Saturday afternoons listening to radio broadcasts from the Metropolitan Opera. At eleven years old, Odetta began taking piano lessons, and one day when she was singing scales with friends, she hit a high C note. Her teacher was amazed and suggested to Odetta's mother that Odetta should take voice lessons, and she did, learning perfect diction and studying classical voice while learning to sing German lieder. Deep down, however, she knew that becoming an opera singer would be next to impossible for a Black woman.

Odetta. *Jac. de Nijs—Anefo/National Archives of the Netherlands (CC BY-SA 3.0 NL) Creative Commons Attribution ShareAlike 3.0 (Netherlands).*

For a time, Odetta attended Los Angeles City College, where she auditioned for a summer stock production of the musical *Finian's Rainbow*, the story of a racist white senator who is transformed into a Black man so that he can experience the sting of Jim Crow laws firsthand. In 1950, Odetta won a part in the play's chorus. The following year, the production moved from Los Angeles to San Francisco, and there, in the coffeehouses of the City by the Bay, Odetta first discovered folk music.

"They were liberation songs," she told *The New York Times*. "You're walking down life's road, society's foot is on your throat, every which way you turn you can't get from under that foot. And you reach a fork in the road and you can either lie down and die or insist upon your life."[2] In a later interview with *Sing Out!* magazine, she elaborated on what the discovery meant to her. "In the songs I heard that night, including prison songs, I found the sadness, the loneliness, the fear that I was feeling at the time. It turned my life around."[3] Borrowing a neighbor's guitar, she began singing these songs that spoke to her and that addressed her anger about America's racism with an incredible intensity and an operatic voice to boot. She also broke with norms of the time, a time when Black women would straighten their hair to conform. Odetta let hers grow out naturally into an Afro.

In the fall of 1956, at twenty-five years old, Odetta searched for a studio where she could record some songs. Even in California, she ran into the same brick wall. Many of the studios had union rules that barred Blacks from recording. Eventually she found a "Jim Crow studio" (one that was manned by Black recording engineers) and recorded sixteen tracks that would become her first solo album, *Odetta Sings Ballads and Blues*.[4] The timing for the release of the album by a small label in New York's Greenwich Village couldn't have been better. Just prior to the release, folk music had gone underground, with many of the singers and songwriters being seen as communists. By the time of the album's release, folk music was ready for a rebirth. The songs swept across the folk music world and influenced many of the genre's future icons, including a young Bob Dylan. "The first thing that turned me on to folk singing was Odetta," he told *Playboy* magazine in 1978, saying that he "heard something vital and personal [in her music]. I learned all the songs on that record."[5]

Odetta used her powerful singing to channel her anger over racism into her work as a political activist. She performed everywhere from small, out-of-the-way coffeehouses to Carnegie Hall and the White House, where she sang for President Kennedy, and at protests, including the Selma to Montgomery march. Her voice and songs became the soundtrack for the Civil Rights Movement. Martin Luther King Jr. called her the queen of American folk music.[6] When asked which songs meant the most to her as a civil rights activist, Rosa Parks replied, "All of the songs Odetta sings."[7]

Throughout her life, Odetta won numerous awards and accolades, including an honorary Doctor of Humane Letters degree from Johnson C. Smith University in Charlotte, North Carolina, and the Duke Ellington Fellowship Award from Yale University. President Bill Clinton presented her with the National Medal of Arts award in 1999, and she was presented with the Living Legend award by the Library of Congress in 2003. Shortly after her death in 2008, dozens of stars gathered at the Riverside Church in Manhattan to pay tribute to her life and legacy. Singer Maria Muldaur was in attendance and summed up the feelings of all in attendance. "I heard the voice of Odetta," she said, "and it changed my life."[8]

---

1. Sasha Frere-Jones, "How Odetta Revolutionized Folk Music," *New Yorker*, February 24, 2022.
2. Tim Weiner, "Odetta, Voice of Civil Rights Movement, Dies at 77," *New York Times*, December 3, 2008.
3. Frere-Jones, "Odetta Revolutionized Folk Music."
4. Ian Zack, "'Odetta Sings Ballads and Blues'—Odetta (1957)," Library of Congress, https://www.loc.gov/static/programs/national-recording-preservation-board/documents/Odetta_Zack.pdf.
5. Weiner, "Odetta."
6. Doug Yeager, "Remembering Odetta, the Voice of the Civil Rights Movement," ASCAP, February 28, 2018, https://www.ascap.com.
7. Weiner, "Odetta."
8. Zack, "Odetta Sings."

Chapter 36

ROSA PARKS

The Mother of the Civil Rights Movement

One of the most iconic figures of the Civil Rights Movement in the 1950s is Tuskegee native Rosa Parks. Her refusal to give up her seat in the front of a Montgomery city bus began a revolution in the city and was a spark that ignited activists around the country who were determined to end racial injustice. Her activism led her to become known as the "mother of the modern civil rights movement."[1]

Rosa was the first child of James and Leona Edwards McCauley. The young family moved from Tuskegee to the small town of Pine Level just north of Montgomery where, at the age of eleven, Rosa was enrolled in the Montgomery Industrial School for Girls, better known as Miss White's School for Girls. The school was established by two white women from the Northeast, Alice White and H. Margaret Beard, in 1886. Their mission was to provide a rigorous Christian education, vocational training and academics for young Black girls from kindergarten to eighth grade. One of the school's founders, Leona McCauley, emphasized time and time again that students should "take advantage of the opportunities, no matter how few they were."[2]

After graduation, Rosa enrolled at the Alabama State Teachers College for Negroes (which later became Alabama State University) but was forced to withdraw to care for her ailing grandmother and then her mother. At nineteen, she met and married a local barber, Raymond Parks. Many people do not realize that long before the famous incident on a Montgomery bus, Rosa was already an activist in the fight against racial injustice. Her husband, Raymond, was already in the fight, and together, the couple began their journey into history. One of their first challenges was to organize the defense of the nine Scottsboro Boys, who were falsely accused of raping two white women in 1931.

For the most part, Rosa and Raymond's activism flew under the radar of most people. In her position with the NAACP, she worked on numerous cases to bring justice to those who had been flogged, murdered or raped. But her pathway to history would begin on August 28, 1955, when fourteen-year-old Emmett Till was abducted and lynched in Mississippi. She later credited that moment and the anger she felt when the killers were not brought to justice with inspiring her to take a stand.[3]

Rosa was a seamstress at the time, and on the evening of December 1, 1955, she had just finished work at the Montgomery Fair Department Store. According to most accounts of the incident in the press, Rosa Parks was an "old woman" who was "tired" after a hard day at work. In her book *My Story*, Rosa took umbrage at this characterization:

> *People always say that I didn't give up my seat because I was tired, but that isn't true. I was not tired physically, or no more tired than I usually was at the end of a working day. I was not old, although some people have an image of me as being old then. I was forty-two. No, the only tired I was, was tired of giving in.*[4]

That night, Rosa climbed on the bus, paid her fare and then realized that the man driving the bus that evening had kicked her off another bus a few years before. Rosa and four other Black passengers took seats in the front rows of the Black section. As the bus continued along its route, it quickly filled with White passengers until some were left standing. Rosa and the other Black passengers would not move from their seats to let the white passengers sit down. The bus driver would not stand for their defiance, saying, "Let me have those front seats." The group didn't move. The driver yelled again, """Y'all better make it light on yourselves and let me have those seats." The other four got up out of their seats and moved farther back in the Black section. Rosa didn't move. She simply slid over next to the window. The driver asked again if she was going to move, and Rosa replied with a simple "No." The driver told her that he would have her arrested. She replied defiantly, "Then you may."[5]

Two policemen were called to the bus and asked Rosa to stand. When she wouldn't, the officer asked why she was refusing, and she stated that she didn't think she should have to. She asked the officer, "Why do they push us [Blacks] around?" He replied, "I don't know, but the law is the law, and you are under arrest."[6] And the rest, as they say, is history. Rosa was charged with disorderly conduct and sent to jail. She was released on bail, which was posted by civil rights leader E.D. Nixon and activists Charles and Virginia Durr. The case went to trial four days later, and Rosa was found guilty and ordered to pay a fourteen-dollar fine.

As pointed out earlier in this book, this was not the first time a Black woman refused to give up her seat on a segregated Montgomery bus. Earlier that year, fifteen-year-old Claudette Colvin was arrested, and two months before Rosa Parks, eighteen-year-old Mary Louise Smith was arrested. Both were charged with the same crime. Neither incident caused a stir like Rosa Parks did when she stood her ground and kept her seat. It was the spark that ignited the 381-day Montgomery Bus Boycott, a protest that would virtually shut down the city's transit system as Black workers found alternative means of transportation. After release, Rosa played a key role in the protest, acting as a dispatcher to coordinate rides for protestors and traveling to address churches and other organizations in the region to raise funds for the protest. Parks was indicted a second time, along with Martin Luther King Jr. and eighty others, for her participation in the boycott.

While Rosa's protest was an important moment for the Civil Rights Movement, it came with consequences. She lost her job and was constantly harassed with death threats. Rosa and Raymond moved to Detroit in 1957, where they continued their fight. There, she became a deaconess in the African Methodist Episcopal (AME) church in 1964 and established the Rosa and Raymond Parks Institute for Self-Development to motivate and direct youth not targeted by other programs to achieve their highest potential.[7] Over her lifetime, she was awarded forty-three honorary doctorates as well as the Congressional Gold Medal of Honor, presented by President Bill Clinton in 1999. Rosa Parks passed away in 2005 at the age of ninety-two, but her legacy lives on.

---

1. "Rosa Louise Parks Biography," Rosa and Raymond Parks Institute, https://www.rosaparks.org.
2. "All Achievers: Rosa Parks, Pioneer of Civil Rights," American Academy of Achievement, June 6, 2019, https://achievement.org.
3. "Rosa Parks," NAACP, May 5, 2021, https://naacp.org.
4. Rosa Parks and James Haskins, *Rosa Parks: My Story* (Perfection Learning, 1999), 116.
5. Parks and Haskins, *My Story*, 114–16.
6. "Rosa Parks, Pioneer," American Academy of Achievement.
7. "Rosa Louise Parks Biography," Rosa and Raymond Parks Institute.

Chapter 37

SIBYL MURPHREE POOL

Opening the Door for Alabama Women in Politics

Sibyl Murphree Pool had one of the most incredible political careers in Alabama. She held several different offices in her thirty-four-year career, opening the door for Alabama women to participate in politics.

Sibyl was born in Birmingham in 1901, and her family moved to Linden, Alabama, shortly thereafter. The second of five children born to Benajamin Franklin and Annie Mae Mills Pool, Sibyl was a bright young woman who went on to attend the Alabama College for Women (today known as the University of Montevallo) from 1920 to 1921. After graduation, she enrolled at the Livingston State Teachers College. She loved to play the violin, and that passion afforded her the opportunity to teach violin lessons at her alma mater, Linden High School.

Her first encounter with politics came in 1923, when she watched her father at work after being elected Marengo County tax collector. Her own public service began in the early 1930s, when she became the director of the Marengo County Farm Bureau and secretary of the Linden Chamber of Commerce. In 1936, while she was working in these positions, the state house representative for the district, Clint Harrison, left his position, and the county Democratic Executive Committee tapped Sibyl to take his place. She was appointed to the position and completed the remaining two years of his term in office. As her time in office expired, Sibyl made the decision to run for the seat, and she was elected for a four-year term not once but twice, in 1938 and 1942, making her the second woman to be elected to the Alabama House of Representatives (the first was suffragist Hattie Hooker Wilkens in 1922).

While in office, Sibyl did not introduce any legislation or debate on the House floor. She maneuvered carefully through her terms so as to not endanger her political ambitions.[1] Her second term in the House was cut short when Governor Chauncey Sparks appointed her secretary of state, a position that had recently opened up with the resignation of Howell Turner, who took over as chairman of the Board of Pardons and Paroles. After she left the statehouse for her new position, another woman would not serve in the legislature until 1962.[2]

As her term in office as secretary of state was ending, Sibyl Pool again decided to make a run to retain the position for a full term, and she won the 1946 election handily, winning sixty-five of Alabama's sixty-seven counties, the largest victory of any candidate in state history, making her the first woman elected to statewide office in Alabama. Pool was elected for a second term four years later and then set her sights on another state office, public service commissioner. In 1954, Sibyl won her first of four terms as PSC, winning all sixty-seven Alabama counties.[3]

Sibyl Murphree Pool retired from politics in 1970 after thirty-four years in public service. She returned to a quiet life on her cattle farm and passed away in 1973. She was inducted into the Alabama Women's Hall of Fame in 2001 for her incredible political career that opened the door for women in Alabama to be a part of state politics. Her political determination was summed up perfectly by one of her hometown newspapers: "The man who said 'a woman's place is in the home' would find it hard sledding to cope with Miss Pool. She doesn't like cooking, sewing, or housekeeping. She'd rather hunt birds and squirrels any day."[4]

---

1. "Sibyl Murphree Pool," Encyclopedia of Alabama, November 1, 2017, https://encyclopediaofalabama.org/
2. "Sibyl Murphree Pool," Encyclopedia of Alabama.
3. "Sibyl Murphree Pool (1901–1973)," Alabama Women's Hall of Fame, http://www.awhf.org.
4. "Sibyl Murphree Pool, First Woman Elected to Statewide Office," Alabama Department of Archives & History, YouTube, 2024, 0:42 to 0:53, https://youtu.be/WUFz6uD5C4Q.

Chapter 38

MARTHA REEVES

Dancing in the Street to Stardom

Once you hear it, you can't get it out of your head: the huge Motown hit record by Martha and the Vandellas, "Dancing in the Street." The group's lead singer, Martha Reeves, has her roots right here in Alabama. Martha's parents, Elijah and Ruby, met in the town of Abbeville, and according to Martha, the couple courted to a perpetual musical soundtrack. "Together they would sit under the moonlight on the big front porch in Abbeville. When Elijah came courting, he would bring his guitar. He would play and sing, and Ruby would join in. [Ruby's] parents would leave them alone as long as they could still hear music coming from the porch."[1] The couple married in June 1937; Ruby was fifteen and Elijah nineteen. Young as they were, they worked hard on a local farm to make ends meet. After they moved to Eufaula, Alabama, their first daughter and third child, Martha Rose Reeves, was born in 1941.

Not long after Martha's birth, farming work began to dwindle, forcing the family to relocate. As many Black families did, they joined the Great Migration north, landing in Detroit in 1942, when Martha was eleven months old. The family moved into a three-bedroom house that they shared with an aunt and an uncle and their families. It was cramped quarters, to say the least. One bedroom was actually a converted closet. Space was at a premium as the family grew in numbers. As Martha later described it, "The family continued to grow one new sibling after another until there were 12 of us in all."[2] Her mother loved the music of Billie Holiday, and even after a hard day working from sunup to sundown and taking care of all the kids, she would sing the children to sleep.

Martha's grandfather was a pastor at the Metropolitan AME Church in Detroit. That's where the Reeves children first began singing in public, and they became the church's choir. In high school, with the encouragement of her vocal teacher, Martha began singing solo under the name Martha Lavaille. Later, she joined up with two friends, Rosalind Ashford and Annette Beard, to form a group, the Del-Phis. The group took first place in a local contest, winning a three-night engagement to sing at Detroit's 20 Grand club. Martha was twenty-one at the time.

As if it was a scene right out of a movie, it just so happened that a man with connections was in the audience: William "Mickey" Stevenson, the arts and repertoire director for Motown Records. Stevenson was so impressed with Martha's voice that he recommended she come to the record company's headquarters, Hitsville U.S.A., and audition. Taking his advice, Martha arrived at the Detroit studio with every intention of auditioning that day, but she immediately ran into an obstacle. A man met her at the door and told her that she needed an appointment. She flashed Stevenson's business card and was allowed in, but as it turned out, the man was correct. When Martha met up with Stevenson, he told her that yes, she needed to make an appointment. It was a very busy day at the studio when Martha walked in, so much so that the phone kept ringing off the hook and no one was available to answer it—so she did, appointing herself Motown's receptionist. Eventually, Martha was given the opportunity to sing but only as a backup singer for other Motown greats, like Marvin Gaye on his hit "Pride and Joy."[3]

One day in 1962, Motown's hit singer Mary Wells ("My Guy") did not show up for a recording session. With an opening in the studio, it was suggested that Martha and her two friends from the Del-Phis step in. Motown founder Barry Gordy was so impressed with the group that he immediately signed them to the label. One notable change was made: the group's name. Martha came up with a new name by combining the name of her favorite street in the city, Van Dyke, and the name of her favorite singer, Della Reese. And with that, Martha and the Vandellas were born. The group scored their first hit when they recorded a song written by what would become the powerhouse songwriting team Holland-Dozier-Holland. It was the first song ever produced by the songwriters, "Come and Get These Memories." The song went to No. 29 on the Billboard Top 40 in 1963 and No. 6 on the R&B charts. The group's biggest hit would come two years later in late 1964.

As Martha recalls, one afternoon around four o'clock, the Vandellas were finishing a music theory class at Motown led by Maurice King. She walked across the street to Hitsville to hear a song that Stevenson had just written. When she arrived, she heard Marvin Gaye sing the first line of the song: "Calling out around the world, are you ready for a brand new beat…" "I was mesmerized," she recalls on her website. "As I stood there in awe of him and his jazzy smooth voice, he glanced my way and said to William Stevenson, 'Let's try this song on Martha.' I was taken aback. I nearly fainted. What a thrill! I had practically memorized the song after listening to Marvin croon it. But I asked if I could sing it the way I felt it. They agreed and I gave it a go."[4]

Martha said the song reminded her of the cobblestone streets where she used to live. She remembered how the street would be blocked off, record players would blare the latest 45 rpm records and the kids in the area would dance in the streets on hot summer nights. "It's a call," she says of the song, "Dancing in the Streets." "[It's] a shout out for the world to dance and celebrate freedom. It will always mean great excitement to me."[5]

The song skyrocketed to No. 2 on the Billboard Hot 100 and became an instant million seller. It was rereleased in the United Kingdom in 1969, reaching No. 4 on the British charts. Since that time, "Dancing in the Streets" has been recorded by many artists, including the rock group Van Halen, the Kinks and the Mamas and the Papas; the most famous cover of the song was recorded by the Rolling Stones' Mick Jagger and David Bowie in 1985. According to Rolling Stones guitarist Keith Richards, the song was the inspiration for the Stones' hit record "Satisfaction."

Since that time, Martha Reeves has won numerous awards, including the Pioneer Award from the Rhythm and Blues Foundation, the Spirit of Detroit Award and the Dick Clark American Soul Award. She was inducted into the Rock 'n Roll Hall of Fame and the Alabama Music Hall of Fame in 1995.

---

1. Martha Reeves, "My Story: My Life Begins," Martha Reeves—Official, https://www.marthareevesofficial.com.
2. Reeves, "My Story."
3. Encyclopedia of Detroit, "Reeves, Martha," Detroit Historical Society, https://detroithistorical.org.
4. Martha Reeves, "Dancing in the Street," Martha Reeves—Official, https://www.marthareevesofficial.com.
5. Reeves, "Dancing."

Chapter 39

CONDOLEEZZA RICE

Mastering Transformational Diplomacy

When it comes to national politics and international affairs, a notable woman from Alabama stands out: Condoleezza Rice. Over her lifetime, Condoleezza has held numerous top positions in the U.S. government dealing with many national security issues, including during the 9/11 attacks.

The Birmingham native was born in 1954, but her ambition in life wasn't to become the nation's first African American secretary of state. Her passion was music, in particular playing piano, and she dreamed of one day becoming a concert pianist. Her love of music came from her grandmother, who taught piano to twenty students for twenty-five cents a session. Condoleezza was fascinated with her piano playing, and when those sessions were over, she would sneak over to the piano, pretend to read the music and play by banging on the keys.[1]

It wasn't long before she could actually read music and play the piano, and following high school graduation, she enrolled at the University of Denver in 1974 as a music major—but after taking one course in political science, her life would change dramatically. She changed her major, graduated with a bachelor's degree in political science and then earned her master's degree from Notre Dame in 1975 and a doctorate from the Graduate School of International Studies of Denver in 1981.

One year after graduating, she accepted the position of assistant professor at Stanford University, teaching political science. From there, Condoleezza's career skyrocketed: she quickly advanced to become the university's first female and first African American provost. During her time as provost, she led the university out of a financial crisis and founded an after-school program for underprivileged children called the Center for a New Generation.[2] But Condoleezza would have a higher calling: to use her knowledge to serve her country. In 1986, Condoleezza was an international affairs fellow at the Council on Foreign Relations, and soon after, she served as special assistant to the director of the Joint Chiefs of Staff. In 1989, she was tapped by President George H.W. Bush to serve on the National Security Council, where she was made the director of Soviet and European affairs.[3]

Condoleezza Rice's abilities showed no limits: in 2001, she was appointed national security advisor by President George W. Bush, and three years later, she became the sixty-sixth American secretary of state and the first African American woman to hold the position, succeeding General Colin Powell. As secretary of state, Rice developed a style of diplomacy she described as "transformational." She sought to redistribute U.S. diplomats to areas of severe social and political trouble; direct the State Department to address worldwide issues, including fighting disease, drug smuggling and human trafficking; and reemphasize aid through the creation of the position of director of foreign assistance.[4] Her most successful negotiations as secretary of state included an agreement for Israel to remove its troops from the country's border with Gaza, allowing the border to reopen, and a ceasefire between Israel and Hezbollah in 2006.[5]

Like many Americans, one of Condoleezza's memories of growing up was the day that President John F. Kennedy was assassinated. It was an image that left an impression on her, and as she recalls in her memoir, for Black Americans in the South, the reaction was fear for their own safety. "Fortunately, though, Lyndon Johnson [President Kennedy's successor] was a southerner. He carried through on Kennedy's promise to end segregation."[6]

Decades later, when she was national security advisor, a request to commemorate the fortieth anniversary of the signing of the Civil Rights Act was brought up in a meeting at the White House. The proposal received a lukewarm reception. In fact, those attending the meeting thought President Bush should simply issue a written statement noting the anniversary. "I hit the roof," she later wrote, "and, more pointedly than perhaps I should have, told my colleagues that they'd better understand that the 1964 act was the one that had made it possible for me to eat in a restaurant in my hometown."[7] The staff was "taken aback," and they relented. A celebration was held in the East Room of the White House with President Johnson's daughter, Lynda Bird Johnson Robb, in attendance. Condoleezza took the moment to thank her personally "for her father's courage and commitment in bringing about dramatic changes in my life." Those changes made an incredible difference in the life of Condoleezza Rice and in the history of the country.

---

1. Condoleezza Rice, *Condoleezza Rice: A Memoir of My Extraordinary, Ordinary Family and Me* (Ember, 2012), 2.
2. Arlisha R. Norwood, "Condoleezza Rice (1954–)," National Women's History Museum, 2017, https://www.womenshistory.org.
3. "Biographies of the Secretaries of State: Condoleezza Rice (1954–)," U.S. Department of State, https://history.state.gov.
4. "Condoleezza Rice," U.S. Department of State.
5. "Condoleezza Rice," U.S. Department of State.
6. Rice, *Memoir*, 8.
7. Rice, *Memoir*, 8.

Chapter 40

SONIA SANCHEZ

Exploring the Black Experience Through Poetry

With her focus on Black life and history and her unique blend of musical genres and African American vernacular English, Sonia Sanchez became one of the most notable poets in America. Born Wilsonia Benita Driver, she hails from Birmingham, the daughter of Wilson and Lena Driver. Her birth name, Wilsonia, was derived from the fact that her parents were not expecting a girl. If the baby were a boy, he would be named after his father; otherwise, they didn't have a name. When their daughter arrived, they decided to add *-ia* to her father's name and came up with Wilsonia, a unique start to a unique life. Later, she would shorten the name and call herself Sonia.

Growing up in Alabama, young Sonia was fascinated by the language of African Americans in the deep South, their melodic and rhythmic pronunciations of words and their dialect, especially that of her grandmother, a woman Sonia grew close to after her mother passed away at an early age. Following her grandmother's death, Wilson Driver moved his family to Harlem in New York City, an area of the Big Apple with a rich and diverse cultural history. Sonia soaked in that culture and its sounds. It was here that she began her literary adventures by reading the works of another Alabama native, Zora Neale Hurston. Hurston promoted the preservation of traditional Black dialects and the cultural heritage of rural Black Southerners, an effort that helped influence the Harlem Renaissance of the 1920s and '30s. Sonia attended many recitals, both poetry and jazz, with her father.[1]

In 1955, Sonia graduated with a bachelor's degree in political science from New York's Hunter College, where she studied poetry under renowned American poet Louise Bogan. Bogan imparted to Sonia her subtle but emotional style of writing, and combined with Sonia's ability to capture the heartbeat of the African American community where she lived, this led to the publication of her own poetry, which appeared in a number of journals published by various writers' workshops in Greenwich Village and the popular *Negro Digest*, which was geared toward literature designed to uplift and educate its African American audience.[2] Her first true solo compilation of poetry was her 1969 book *Home Coming*, described in *Poetry Magazine* as an "attack on the exploitation of African Americans in racially charged America during the 1960s."[3]

Around this time (the late 1960s), Sonia married Puerto Rican immigrant Albert Sanchez. It was a short marriage, however. They divorced, and she then married Etheridge Knight in 1968, choosing to keep her first husband's surname, Sanchez. The couple had three children, and the marriage ended in divorce by 1972.

Sonia's involvement in the Civil Rights Movement began while she was teaching classes at a number of institutions in the New York area, including Manhattan Community College and Amherst College. She was also a faculty advisor for students. Sonia recalled the day she and the students she was advising walked into the school president's office and made a series of demands to improve the life of the students.

> *In came the police, and we were arrested. They put me in a cell with the ladies of the night. The judge said if I didn't do anything wrong in the next six months, it wouldn't be on my record. The president of the school was so angry. I went looking for another teaching job, but I couldn't find one. Finally, someone I knew at the education department told me, "They don't intend to let you teach."*[4]

Sonia became a member of the activist group CORE (Congress of Racial Equality) and staged numerous protests in the city, including shutting down 135th Street in an attempt to force unions into hiring Black and Puerto Rican men. Then one day, a note came that read, "Whatever you do, you'll have to include me, because I *am* Harlem." It was from the civil rights activist Malcolm X. She disagreed with some of Malcolm X's ideas about how to change society and even told him so. "I told him I didn't agree with some of what he said. But his eyes were so gentle. And he looked at me and said, 'One day you will, my sister.'"[5]

In 1977, Sonia accepted a teaching position at Temple University in Philadelphia, where she remained until her retirement in 1977. Among the awards and accolades Sonia Sanchez has received over the years, she was awarded an honorary doctorate from Trinity College in 1988, presented with the Distinguished Minority Faculty Fellowship at Delaware University in 1987 and received an award from the Women's International League for Peace and Freedom in 1988. After she moved to Philadelphia, she became the city's first poet laureate, serving from 2012 to 2014.

As of this writing, Sonia has written over twenty books of poetry, her most famous being 1984's *Homegirls and Hand Grenades*, which won her the 1984 American Book Award. She also continues to hold her unique readings where audience members immerse themselves in her rhythmic stylings, often clapping along and loudly replying to her callouts.

---

1. "Zora Neale Hurston," Encyclopedia of Alabama, April 21, 2008, https://encyclopediaofalabama.org.
2. "Sonia Sanchez," Poetry Foundation, November 19, 2024, https://www.poetryfoundation.org.
3. "Sonia Sanchez," Poetry Foundation.
4. Victor Fiorillo, "Sonia Sanchez Still Has Work to Do," *Philadelphia Magazine*, February 20, 2021, https://www.phillymag.com.
5. Fiorillo, "Sonia Sanchez."

Chapter 41

RUBY PICKENS TARTT

Alabama Folklorist and Painter

If you've ever heard audio recordings from the 1930s of former slaves singing work and religious songs or retelling their often horrifying life stories, chances are those recordings were the work of famed Alabama folklorist Ruby Pickens Tartt. Ruby was born in Livingston, Alabama, in Sumter County in 1880, only fifteen years removed from the Civil War. It was a time when old plantations were being divided into parcels of land and former slaves (tenants) were allowed to work the land, paying the landowner back with a portion of the proceeds from their harvest.

The landowners in Sumter County took an interest in the welfare of their tenants. Most landowners knew each of them by name, visited their churches and attended their funerals. They even came out to the fields and would check on the workers to see if they needed anything, maybe some water or something to eat. And that is how Ruby Pickens became so passionate about preserving this culture. Her father was a prosperous cotton farmer and landowner, and she loved traveling with him to the fields and talking with the tenants. It was there that her appreciation of African American culture—its stories and its songs—took root. On one of her trips to the fields, she first heard the voices of Adele "Vera" Hall and Doc Reed. Her encounter with Reed made a deep impression on her; his voice was rich, she said, and "sounded out from the group like a trumpet call."[1]

Ruby jotted down on paper the tenants' stories and songs, but as a teenager attending the Alabama Normal School (today known as the University of West Alabama), documenting the songs and stories of former Black slaves wasn't her calling—not yet, anyway. Her focus was on becoming a painter. She studied painting at the Alabama Normal School and then transferred to Sophia Newcomb College in New Orleans. Finally, in 1901, she attended the William Chase School of Art in New York City.

It was while attending Chase that Ruby met Professor Carl Cramer. Cramer was a professor of English and shared many of Ruby's interests, especially in preserving the African American experience in the South. Cramer recalled his first meeting with Ruby: "I was drenched in a shower of proverbs, spells, superstitions, recipes, descriptions of all-day-singings-with-dinner-on-the-grounds, county barbecues, fiddlers' conventions, ballads of old crimes, tales of Brer Rabbit and Sis Cow, baptisms, spirituals, [and] poetic quotations from Negro preachers."[2] Cramer was so drawn into Ruby's stories that he decided to send his notes on her recollections to an Alabama scholarly journal. When he told her his plans, she proposed that he author a book instead of simply publishing notes in a journal. He did, and the result was the highly acclaimed book *Stars Fell on Alabama*, which was published in 1934 and launched Cramer's writing career. The book's fictional main character, Mary Louise, was based on Ruby.

Following graduation, Ruby returned to Alabama and married a well-to-do banker from Livingston, William Pratt Tartt, in 1904. With financial security, Ruby was free to explore her passion for painting while continuing to chronicle the stories of African Americans in rural Alabama. She would drive around dusty clay roads with pen, notepad and her art supplies in a car that was a gift from her father, believed to be one of the first cars in the state, with the goal of preserving this rich history.[3]

Ruby Tartt outside her home in Livingston, Alabama. *Library of Congress Prints and Photographs Division.*

All was well with Ruby and William until 1929, when the stock market crash and the Great Depression decimated the family's wealth, but Ruby's work would be to the couple's benefit. Her work chronicling the African American experience was becoming widely known across the region, and in 1936, she was appointed the chair of the Federal Writers' Project in Sumter County. The FWP was part of President Roosevelt's

New Deal Works Progress Administration (WPA) program. Her mission was the same as it was prior to the appointment: chronicle African American life in rural Alabama. Her prior experiences gave her unique access to these formerly enslaved people who had grown to trust her over the years.

Soon, Ruby's work crossed the desk of musicologist and folklorist John Lomax. Lomax was assigned by the FWP to join Ruby on the road to make audio recordings of the singers and storytellers in order to preserve their voices for posterity. Ruby and John quickly became close friends as they drove out to the many farms dotting the landscape. Since many of the farms had no electricity, Ruby shuttled the families to her home, where they recorded their stories and songs. Sometimes she would pay the workers for their time, but she always made sure they were fed. If Lomax had to record remotely, he had a special setup in the trunk of his car with two car batteries that could power the recorders.[4]

One of the most famous recordings the team made was of a woman Ruby had heard sing in her earlier travels: Adele "Vera" Hall. Lomax was immediately captivated by Hall's voice, describing it as coming "from deep within her…from a source of gold and light, otherwise hidden, [that] falls directly upon your ear like sunlight."[5]

Ruby passed away in 1974, but those recordings and the thousands of manuscripts she produced are still pored over by scholars and historians around the world. Ruby was inducted into the Alabama Women's Hall of Fame in 1980 as one of the country's foremost chroniclers of African American culture.

---

1. Virginia Pounds Brown and Laurella Owens, *Toting the Lead Row: Ruby Pickens Tartt, Alabama Folklorist* (University of Alabama Press, 1981), 18.
2. Carl Carmer, *Miss Ruby, My Most Unforgettable Character* (Livingston University Press, 1975), 3.
3. Peter Stone and Ellen Harold, "Ruby Pickens Tartt," Association for Cultural Equity, https://www.culturalequity.org.
4. Stephanie Hall, "Alabama Folklorist Ruby Pickens Tartt," *Library of Congress Blogs*, January 12, 2019, https://blogs.loc.gov.
5. "Vera Ward Hall," Lomax Digital Archive.

Chapter 42

WILLIE MAE "BIG MAMA" THORNTON

Bridging the Gap Between Blues and Rock 'n Roll

It's not difficult to trace the roots of American rock 'n roll music. It began with the blues, a fusion of religious and work songs sung by African Americans in the South in the early twentieth century. There was one person who has been considered the bridge builder between the blues and rock music: Alabama's own Wille Mae "Big Mama" Thornton.

Willie Mae was born in the small town of Ariton near Montgomery to George W. and Mattie Haynes Thornton in 1926. Her father was a Baptist minister, her mother a housewife. When she was four, her family, which included five siblings, moved to nearby Troy City. The young Wille Mae loved music and taught herself to play drums. She also learned how to play harmonica by watching her brother, "Caliope" Thornton, play the harp. She would dig his old harmonicas out of the trash when he threw them away.[1] She also loved to sing, a passion she developed watching her mother, Mattie, sing in her father's church choir.

Her early years in school were difficult for Willie Mae. First of all, she was very tall, and her classmates mocked her for it. She would hunch down, trying to make herself as small as possible, but to no avail.[2] Then her mother became very ill, suffering from tuberculosis, which forced Willie Mae to miss classes to help care for her. By the age of thirteen, Willie Mae had made it only to the third grade. That same year, her mother, Mattie, passed away, and Willie Mae left school to find a job to support her family.

This is where the story of Willie Mae Thornton gets a little cloudy. Some accounts say that she found a job cleaning spittoons at a local tavern. When the bar's house vocalist showed up one day so drunk she couldn't perform, Willie Mae convinced the owner to let her sing.[3] Another says that she won a talent contest at the age of fourteen and the prize was a chance to sing with a troupe called Sammy Green's Hot Harlem Revue. A third account says that a singer by the name of Diamond Teeth Mary heard Thornton sing and hooked her up with Sammy Green's Hot Harlem Revue. She did travel with Green for ten years as a singer, drummer, comedian and harmonica player, so that much is true.[4]

No matter the real story about how Willie Mae was discovered—her career had been launched. Early on, she earned the nickname Big Mama. That was partly due to how tall she was, but mostly it was for her voice, which was brash, growly and powerful. It is said that her voice was big enough to overwhelm a packed auditorium. Her travels with the Hot Harlem Revue took her across the country, playing such notable venues as the Cotton Club in Harlem and small, long-forgotten juke joints in the bayous of the Deep South—called the Chitlin' Circuit by performers. Big Mama wowed crowds at every stop with her brilliant comedy and mesmerizing harmonica playing. Even her appearance made a big statement. "She was what one writer called a gender transgressor," blues musician Erica Brown wrote of Big Mama. "She did not let the world tell her how to dress, who to be, how to sing, or how to live her life."[5] She was well known for taking to the stage wearing a flannel shirt, jacket and slacks or dungarees like male blues singers.

During one performance, the (at the time) unknown songwriting team of Lieber and Stoller heard Big Mama and decided to write a song for her. It would be their first of many hit songs and the one that put Big Mama on the national radar. The song was called "Hound Dog." It would become Big Mama's first and only No. 1 record, topping the Billboard R&B chart in 1953 and remaining there for fourteen weeks. The song caught the ear of a young, up-and-coming rock star, Elvis Presley, who recorded the song himself. The record became the King's biggest hit, reaching No. 1 in 1956, propelling him to rock stardom. After hearing the Elvis version, Big Mama commented that rock 'n roll was "just the blues speeded up." Indeed it was.

Unfortunately for Big Mama, the record industry at the time was not kind to artists, especially Black artists. According to Big Mama, when her version of "Hound Dog" hit No. 1, "I got one check for $500 and I never seen another." Another song, "Ball and Chain," was written and recorded by Big Mama. The record had fairly good success on the charts, but again, she never saw royalties from it. Even when rock icon Janis Joplin recorded the song, which became almost an anthem of hers, Big Mama did not receive a single dime in royalties.

Willie Mae "Big Mama" Thornton never did reach star status, but over her forty-four-year career, in which she wrote more than twenty songs and recorded several albums, her influence shaped the face of rock 'n roll and the blues. Stars including the Rolling Stones' Mick Jagger, Queen's Freddie Mercury and many others attribute a part of their success to Big Mama. The popularity of the blues slowly died out toward the end of the 1960s, replaced by rock. Big Mama began to drink heavily, and it began to affect her health. She died in 1984. In 2020, she was inducted into the Alabama Music Hall of Fame, and in 2024, she made it into the Rock 'n Roll Hall of Fame in Cleveland.

---

1. Michael Sporke, *Big Mama Thornton: The Life and Music* (McFarland, 2014), 6.
2. Sporke, *Big Mama Thornton*, 6–7.
3. Sporke, *Big Mama Thornton*, 7.
4. Maureen Mahon, "'Big Mama' Thornton: Her Songs, Sound, Style, and Attitude Made Formative Contributions to the Development of Rock 'n Roll," Rock 'n Roll Hall of Fame, https://rockhall.com.
5. Elle Naef, "Local Blues Legends Honor Big Mama Thornton's Legacy," Rocky Mountain PBS, December 11, 2023, https://www.rmpbs.org.

Chapter 43

JULIA S. TUTWILER

Angel of the Stockades

Driving up US Highway 231 in Wetumpka, you will pass an unassuming white building, the Julia Tutwiler Prison for Women. The facility was named for one of the most noted educators and crusaders for prison reform in Alabama, Julia S. Tutwiler.

Julia was the daughter of Henry and Julia Tutwiler. Her father was the head of the Ancient Languages Department at the University of Alabama and was very progressive in his beliefs. From an early age, Julia's father told her that "women were the educational equals of men and should be treated as such."[1] The family sent Julia off to boarding school in Philadelphia, where she learned music, art and several languages. She then attended the all-female Vassar College in Poughkeepsie, New York, in 1866 as part of the college's first class, but finances prevented her from completing her education, and she returned to Alabama, where she began teaching at the Greensboro Female Academy.[2]

Her education continued through the mid-1870s as she traveled to Europe and attended schools in Prussia and authored articles for *St. Nicholas Magazine* and *Appleton's Journal* before returning to teaching in Alabama. She went on to help establish the Alabama Normal College for Girls (later known as the University of West Alabama) and the University of Montevallo. Fueled by her father's belief that women are the intellectual equals of men, Julia became the president of Livingston State Normal School, where she earned the moniker "Mother of Co-Education in Alabama" as she led the fight to allow ten girls admission to the University of Alabama.

Julia S. Tutwiler. *Birmingham Public Library Archives.*

What Julia Tutwiler is most remembered for—and the reason a women's prison is named after her—is her devotion to reforming the state's prisons. In 1879, she organized the Tuscaloosa Benevolent Association (TBA), composed of women who worked to change the rules and conditions in prisons. Julia, known as the "Angel of Prisons" or the "Angel of the Stockades," brought major changes to the prison system, including the separation of male and female prisoners. Up until that time, the sexes were jailed together. She also fought and won the battle to separate juvenile offenders from adults, a victory that resulted in the creation of the first Boys' Industrial School. And along with the TBA, she called for, and won, better prison sanitation and more educational opportunities for inmates.

As the new century rolled around, Julia found herself the president of the Alabama Normal College. In 1910, the college was placed under state control. The new board of trustees accused her of poor financial recordkeeping at the college and of mixing her own personal money with the college's. As a result, they forced her to resign her position. Students were outraged and began a letter-writing campaign that only antagonized the board to the point that they denied her pension.[3]

Another contribution Julia Tutwiler made to the state was to craft a poem titled "Alabama." Written in 1868, the poem was turned into a song, which was adopted as the official state song in 1931.

Julia S. Tutwiler died of cancer in 1916, leaving $15,000 from her estate to the Livingston Normal College to use for scholarships. She was among the first group of women to be inducted into the Alabama Women's Hall of Fame when it was opened in 1970 at Judson College in Marion, Alabama. In 2001, she was inducted into the Tuscaloosa County Civic Hall of Fame, the first year the county's Chamber of Commerce inducted citizens into the hall that honors citizens who made significant, long-term contributions to the development of the county while celebrating the county's history and heritage.[4]

---

1. Jerry Aldridge, Jennifer L. Kilgo, Grace Jepkemboi and Rose Ruto-Korir, "Forgotten Fathers and Mothers: Rethinking the History and Parentage of Progressive Education," *Education, Practice, and Innovation* 1, no. 2 (June 2014): 129.
2. Aldridge et al., "Forgotten Fathers," 129.
3. "Julia S. Tutwiler, 'The Upton Sinclair Fast Cure of the Mind,'" University of Alabama School of Law, https://library.law.ua.edu.
4. "Julia Strudwick Tutwiler, 1841–1916," Tuscaloosa Area Virtual Museum, https://tavm.omeka.net.

Chapter 44

LURLEEN BURNS WALLACE

Alabama's First Female Governor

Following the resignation of Alabama Governor Robert Bentley, on April 10, 2017, Lieutenant Governor Kay Ivey was sworn in as the state's second female governor. Ivey would go on to be reelected two times to the position. Ivey's political ambitions began when she worked on the 1966 gubernatorial campaign of the woman who would become the first female governor of the state: Lurleen B. Wallace.

Lurleen Brigham Burns was born and raised in Tuscaloosa, Alabama. Her father, Henry, worked on barges along the busy Black Warrior River that coursed through the northern part of the state and then, later, as a crane operator in the state's Port City, Mobile, during World War II. One of Lurleen's favorite pastimes as a child was going hunting and fishing with her father, a passion she nurtured throughout her life.

The young Lurleen attended Tuscaloosa Business College, and after graduation, she began working as a clerk at a local Tuscaloosa five-and-dime. It was here that the sixteen-year-old Lurleen Burns met her future husband, George C. Wallace. The twenty-two-year-old Wallace was a recent graduate of the University of Alabama School of Law. In 1943, the couple married. From early on, it was obvious that Lurleen was quite happy with her role as a housewife and mother of four children. George, on the other hand, was all about politics. In 1946, he won the first of two terms in the Alabama House of Representatives, followed by his election as the state circuit judge for the Third District.[1] But Wallace had his eyes on a bigger prize: the governorship.

George Wallace was defeated in his first run for the office in 1958 but made a successful bid during the 1962 election. Lurleen was lukewarm about her role as the state's first lady. Not one for formal functions, she still played the role with dignity and grace, wearing smart dress suits by day and hunting pants by night. But it was her genuine personality, her sincerity and the fact that she came from humble beginnings that made the people of Alabama adore her.[2] As first lady, she refused to serve alcohol at public functions, and as a show of her relationship with the public, she opened the first floor of the governor's mansion for public tours seven days a week.[3]

As her husband's gubernatorial term came to an end, George Wallace wanted to run for a second term. Alabama law, however, prohibited a sitting governor from running for two consecutive terms. Wallace attempted to have the state constitution amended, but when that failed, he resorted to plan B. It started out as an inside joke that quickly became reality: his wife, Lurleen, would run for governor, and George would be her "advisor" and continue making administrative policy.[4] The more they talked about the idea, the more Lurleen grew to like it, and she decided to go for it. During the early days of her campaign, the quiet and demure wife of the governor would begin each rally by saying a few words and then let her husband take over and run the show. Soon, however, she became quite comfortable in her role and was able to address important issues, even ad-libbing lines at rallies.

In the 1966 primary, Lurleen won handily, defeating nine other Democrats including the highly popular former governor "Big Jim" Folsom. She then went on to defeat the most popular Republican in the state, U.S. Congressman Jim Martin, with 57 percent of the vote: a historic margin of two to one.[5] Lurleen Wallace was sworn in as the state's forty-sixth governor on January 15, 1967. For her inauguration, Lurleen refused to have an inaugural ball to show respect for the Alabama servicemen fighting in Vietnam.

While in office, she did follow some of her husband's policy advice, such as resisting the racial integration of schools, but she took her role as governor seriously and had her own agenda. Shortly after the inauguration, she toured a state mental hospital in Tuscaloosa County and was visibly shaken by the horrendous conditions she witnessed. She went to work and gave a powerful speech to the state legislature that convinced lawmakers to deliver a bond issue to support improving mental health care and the state's mental health hospitals. Lurleen was also a key figure in the creation of a major cancer research center at the University of Alabama–Birmingham and a $160 million roads project bill. After visiting newly developed state parks in Kentucky, she set up a program to improve Alabama's aging state parks and historic sites and open new ones.

Two years before she was elected, Lurleen was diagnosed with cancer. By April 1968, her health was in serious decline, and her doctors gave her strict orders not to travel, but she couldn't sit still and would still frequent her favorite getaway in the state, the governor's mansion on the Gulf Coast in the town of Gulf Shores. Lurleen Wallace was not able to complete her term in office, passing away on May 6, 1968. Thousands attended the viewing in the Alabama capitol building's rotunda. Even the Poor People's Campaign, an organization seeking equal rights for Black Americans, postponed a planned protest in the state capital as a sign of respect for Alabama's first female governor.[6]

---

1. "Lurleen B. Wallace (1967–68)," Encyclopedia of Alabama, August 28, 2008, https://encyclopediaofalabama.org.
2. "Lurleen B. Wallace," Encyclopedia of Alabama.
3. "Governor Lurleen B. Wallace," National Governors Association, January 1, 2018, https://www.nga.org.
4. "Governor Lurleen B. Wallace," National Governors Association.
5. "Governor Lurleen B. Wallace," National Governors Association.
6. "Lurleen B. Wallace," Encyclopedia of Alabama.

Chapter 45

DINAH WASHINGTON

The Queen of the Blues

She was called the Queen of the Blues, and while Tuscaloosa native Ruth Lee Jones—better known to the world by her stage name, Dinah Washington—could belt out the blues, she was also one of the most versatile vocalists in American history. She was just as comfortable singing gospel, jazz, rhythm and blues and pop as she was with the blues. As her longtime producer Quincy Jones said of her, Dinah "could take the melody in her hand, hold it like an egg, crack it open, fry it, let it sizzle, reconstruct it, put the egg back in the box and back in the refrigerator and you would've still understood every single syllable."[1]

It was August 29, 1924, when Ruth Lee Jones was born to Ollie and Asalea Williams Jones. Her father, Ollie, was a laborer for a timber company; her mother sang, played piano and taught music at Elizabeth Baptist Church. When Ruth was three years old, the family moved to Chicago, and that is where her love of music took root. Her mother continued her music ministry at the city's St. Luke's Baptist Church and began giving her daughter vocal lessons and teaching her to play piano. By eleven years old, Ruth was a gospel singer and was singing at recitals across the country. When Ruth was fifteen, she took first place in a talent contest held at the Chicago Regal Theater. Her prize was to play piano and sing at several nightclubs in the area. For a while, she split her time singing in a gospel choir and performing in nightclubs, but before long, she dropped the choir.

To say her life was turbulent would be an understatement. It has been confirmed that Ruth married eight times over her lifetime, with the possibility of a ninth marriage. Her first marriage came in 1942 when she was seventeen years old, to twenty-three-year-old John Young. She divorced him three months later.[2] And that is how all her marriages went for the rest of her life. If it lasted more than a year, it was an accomplishment.

In 1943, talent agent Joe Glaser heard Ruth's incredible talent and brought her to the attention of the "King of the Vibes," Lionel Hampton. Best known for his amazing vibraphone playing and his big-band orchestra, Hampton was taken with her penetrating high-pitched voice and vocal range, how clearly she enunciated every word and her sense of timing and drama: she could take a song and make it sad, bawdy, celebratory or rousing, allowing her to sing anything and everything.[3] He was so impressed that he signed her on to sing with the band full time.

How Ruth Lee Jones became Dinah Washington is still a bit of a mystery. One story says her manager gave her the name, while others say it was Hampton. Either way, Dinah Washington was an immediate success and performed with Hampton's band for the next four years. The same year she joined the band, she recorded her first record, "Evil Gal Blues," which went to No. 1 on the Billboard R&B chart. Dinah never looked back, dominating the R&B chart through to the 1950s.

As the 1950s rolled around, Dinah was not only recording blues but also jazz and embarked on singing ballads, with lush orchestration provided by famed musician, orchestra leader and music producer Quincy Jones. "Every single melody she sang," Jones said of Washington, "she made hers. Once she put her soulful trademark on a song, she owned it, and it was never the same." It was with Jones and his orchestra that Dinah recorded her tenth and most popular album, *What a Difference a Day Makes*. The album's title track went on to win a Grammy in 1959 for Best Rhythm and Blues Performance. In all, from 1949 to 1955, Dinah Washington would score twenty-seven top ten hits.

Dinah's life continued to be a turbulent one. The goddaughter of one of Dinah's accompanists, Patti Austin, remembered her personality: "She might have thrown instruments at musicians, but she could easily shower them with presents."[4] Dinah battled weight problems, which resulted in her using a variety of weight loss medications. She was also frivolous with her money, blowing through her newfound wealth by buying expensive shoes, furs and cars. The lifestyle eventually caught up to her much too soon: at the age of thirty-nine, Dinah Washington died from an overdose of a deadly mix of pills. It was a tragic end to a brilliant career, but the incredible music Dinah Washington left us lives on. Dinah was inducted into the Alabama Music Hall of Fame in 1986 and the Rock 'n Roll Hall of Fame in 1993.

---

1. Bob Craig, "Queen of the Blues and Then Some: In Awe of Dinah Washington at 100," WRTI Radio, August 22, 2024, https://www.wrti.org.
2. "Dinah Washington," Encyclopedia of Alabama, https://encyclopediaofalabama.org.
3. "Dinah Washington: August 29, 1924–December 14, 1963, 1991 Inductee," Alabama Music Hall of Fame, https://www.alamhof.org.
4. Jumoke Fashola, "Celebrating Dinah Washington's Centenary," Everything Jazz, August 29, 2024, https://www.everythingjazz.com.

Chapter 46

MARIA HOWARD WEEDEN

The Gentle Artist

Maria Howard Weeden, or simply Howard, was an internationally renowned artist from Huntsville. She had the unique ability to capture images and people she saw in incredible detail, which art historians have called as close to photorealistic as possible, and she did it with a slight handicap—poor vision.

Born on July 6, 1846, in Huntsville, Howard was the daughter of Dr. William Donaldson and Jane Eliza Brooks Urquhart Weeden. Sadly, she never had the chance to meet her father, who passed while returning from a trip to New Orleans six months before she was born. At the time of her birth, Howard and her mother lived in what would later be known as the Weeden House, a mansion built in 1819 on Huntsville's Gates Avenue. The house was occupied by a future associate justice of the U.S. Supreme Court, John McKinley, and a future president of Huntsville Bank, Bartley Lowe, before the Weeden family purchased it in 1845. Howard lived there her entire life. The home is now a museum and open to the public for tours.[1]

Howard had the uncanny ability to capture, in paintings and sketches, the essence of her subject. Her images of flowers captured the finest details, and her portraits of people brought their personalities to life. What is amazing is that she had very poor vision and was legally blind. To work, she positioned her subjects only three inches away from her face.

During the Civil War, when the Union army captured Huntsville, the Weeden home was confiscated and used to house soldiers. The family was forced to move, and they landed in Tuskegee, where they stayed with her older sister, Kate. While there, Howard attended Tuskegee Female Methodist College. When the family returned to Huntsville after the war, they were horrified to find their home ransacked. With little money left,

Howard began teaching art classes and creating paintings and hand-painted notecards, wedding booklets, dinner cards and more to help support the family. She also began writing poems and essays for the *Christian Observer* under the penname Flake White—a nod to her painting, as flake white is a pigment used in paint—which she continued to write for twenty years.[2]

The turning point in her career came in 1893, when she attended the World's Columbian Exposition in Chicago. There, she examined the work of other artists, some of whom attempted to paint and draw former slaves. To Howard, the images were disrespectful caricatures of their subjects, and she knew she could do better, drawing the freed slaves with dignity. Returning to Huntsville, she offered any former slave she knew the opportunity to have their portrait made. It got to the point that many were coming to her asking to have their image sketched. Her portraits gained international recognition when, in 1895, several of her paintings were taken to an art gallery in Germany by her close friend and the president of the Tuskegee Female Methodist College, George Price. The event was called the Howard Weeden Gala. The paintings received such high praise that she received a substantial number of orders for her work. A similar show in Paris resulted in the same acclaim.[3]

Howard wrote four books of poetry in her life, all of which she illustrated herself. The poems were written in the Black dialect of the day and were all based on the stories she heard from the freed slaves she painted. She had the books published under the name Howard Weeden, knowing full well that she would have an easier time selling them than if she used her first name, Maria, in the male-dominated literary world. The first collection of her poems, *Shadows on the Wall*, was published by Boston-based M. Stolz and Company in 1898. Three other collections followed: *Bandanna Ballads* (1899), *Songs of the Old South* (1901) and *Old Voices* (1904).

Maria Howard Weeden continued painting until her death in 1905 from tuberculosis, creating a collection of highly detailed paintings of wildflowers she found on Huntsville's Monte Sano Mountain and of the many varieties of roses found in her mother's garden that appeared in a book titled *The Book of Roses*. Howard was inducted into the Alabama Women's Hall of Fame in 1998.

---

1. "Welcome to the Weeden House," Weeden House Museum, https://www.weedenhousemuseum.com/about-us.html.
2. "Maria Howard Weeden," Encyclopedia of Alabama, https://encyclopediaofalabama.org.
3. "Maria Howard Weeden (1846–1905)," Alabama Women's Hall of Fame, http://www.awhf.org.

Chapter 47

HEATHER WHITESTONE

An Inspiring Journey to National Royalty

It's a parent's worst nightmare: your child comes down with an illness that rapidly worsens to the point of becoming a life-and-death situation. The doctors have no choice but to give your child antibiotics that could either save their life or have adverse consequences. The drugs are administered, and your child survives—but then those "adverse consequences" appear.

That is what happened to the daughter of Daphne Whitestone, Heather, as Daphne found out on Christmas Day 1974. But in an amazing story of love and determination, Daphne helped her daughter become a thriving young woman who would make history despite her disability—being crowned Miss America 1994.

Heather was born in Dothan, Alabama, in 1973, the daughter of Daphne and Bill Whitestone. At only eighteen months old, Heather came down with influenza. Her fever was mild at first but quickly climbed to 104 degrees, and she was rushed to the hospital. Heather was near death when doctors gave her two antibiotics. They warned her parents that they could have serious consequences: blindness, retardation or deafness.

After spending two weeks in the hospital, Heather was sent back home even though she still had an active infection, one serious enough that she was unable to walk and could not feed herself. Her family had to do everything for her. Eventually, her motor skills did return, but on Christmas Day 1974, the family realized that something else was wrong. While her mother, Daphne, was working in the kitchen, she dropped some pots and pans, causing a racket that startled everyone in the house who had gathered for the holiday. Heather was sitting playing by the Christmas tree. Her aunt, who had been watching Heather play, began shouting, "Daphne! I think there's something wrong with Heather's hearing!" Grabbing a pot and a spoon, Daphne rushed up behind Heather and started banging them together. Heather did not move. She didn't hear the noise her mother was making.[1] Heather was fully deaf in one ear and had 5 percent hearing in the other. Doctors insisted that Heather's disability would greatly hamper her education and she would never make it past third grade, but Daphne was not going to let that happen.

"After the doctor told her I would not go past the third grade," Heather told *The New York Times* in 1994, "my mother made the decision for me to speak, and she spent hours working with me on my speech and my schoolwork. She never let me use my deafness as an excuse. We had a positive environment, where if you fail, just try again."[2]

Daphne enrolled Heather in ballet lessons, hoping that the rhythm of the music and movement would help her improve the rhythm of her speech. The idea was for Heather to learn to count the beats in the music, the rhythm, and then do the same with her voice when speaking, counting syllables. The idea worked. In fact, Heather did not learn sign language until she was in high school, preferring to speak instead of sign. "It is best for me to speak," she told *The New York Times*, "but that's for me. It doesn't bother me to sign. It's a beautiful language....I remember I gave testimony at the church once, and I meant to talk about being baptized, and I signed 'dead.' Oh, no!"[3]

But speech wasn't the only way Heather communicated. She had also fallen in love with ballet. To her, "the dancers communicated with body language. Words weren't necessary."[4]

There was one time that Heather said she was glad she was deaf. She had a hearing aid, and one night, her sister Melissa woke her up at two o'clock in the morning complaining that she couldn't sleep because their father was snoring. Heather turned on her hearing aid, heard how horrible the sound was, turned it back off, said, "Too bad" and went back to sleep.[5]

When Heather was a teenager, things began to move quickly for her. She graduated from Berry High School in 1991, and following an audition with ballerina Sonia Aroya, who had danced with Rudolph Nureyev, she was admitted to the Alabama School of Fine Arts. Heather decided to compete in the Junior Miss Pageant. During the competition, she was so helpful to her fellow contestants that she won the pageant's Spirit Award and a scholarship, which she used to attend college at Jacksonville State University. In 1992, she competed in the college's Miss Jacksonville State pageant and won free tuition for one semester. When she was announced as the winner, she didn't know until another contestant tapped her on the shoulder and told her.

Three months later, Heather made another decision: to compete in the Miss Alabama Pageant, a stepping stone to competing in the Miss America pageant. She entered in 1992 and 1993, coming in first runner-up both times. But as they say, the third time's the charm, and she was off to Atlantic City. Heather was to compete in the talent competition by performing a ballet routine. The obvious question is: How could someone perform a flawless ballet if they are deaf? Besides, pageant rules forbid contestants having assistance from their coaches. For two years, Heather practiced a ballet routine to Sandi Pattie's song "Via Delarosa." She counted the beats with her hands, memorizing the rhythm so she could time her movements. When the music started, she performed the dance by counting the beats in her head.[6] And it was a flawless performance.

As the 1995 Miss America pageant drew to a close, only two finalists remained: Miss Virginia, Cullen Johnson, and Heather Whitestone. When host Regis Philbin announced that Heather was the new Miss America, there was a moment when she didn't realize what had just happened, but then Cullen Johnson pointed at her excitedly, and Heather's reign as Miss America began.

In one of her first interviews, a *New York Times* reporter asked if she had any plans to be married. "Eventually," she replied. "But only to a one-woman man. An honest person and also a Christian." And she did. While serving on President Clinton's Committee on Employment of People with Disabilities, she met her future husband, David McCallum, at the Capitol, and they were married in 1996. The couple have four children and currently live in Georgia.

During her reign as Miss America, Heather devoted her time to working with deaf children and teaching them that positive thinking is the key to success and overcoming any disability and obstacle. After her time wearing the crown, she became a spokesperson for the Helen Keller Eye Research Foundation and authored four books, including her autobiography and devotional titles like *Believing the Promise*.

---

1. Heather Whitestone, *Listening with My Heart* (Doubleday, 1996), 2–4.
2. Alex Witchel, "Going Home With: Heather Whitestone; Placing the Person Ahead of the Crown," *New York Times*, October 27, 1994.
3. Witchel, "Going Home."
4. Whitestone, *Listening with My Heart*, 8.
5. Whitestone, *Listening with My Heart*, 10.
6. Marta Belsky, "Living Loud: Heather Whitestone—First Deaf Miss America," Signing Savvy, September 16, 2014, https://www.signingsavvy.com.

Chapter 48

HATTIE HOOKER WILKINS

The First Woman Elected to the Alabama State Legislature

Earlier, you read the story of Sibyl Murphree Poole, the first woman elected to statewide office in Alabama. Sibyl was also the second woman elected to the state house of representatives. But her being second woman means that there had to be a first, and that would be Hattie Hooker Wilkins.

The Selma, Alabama native was born in 1875, the daughter of Frederick Josiah and Alexina Fellows Hooker. Hattie excelled in school, attending Bass Calloway's School in Selma and then the Peabody Normal College in Nashville, from which she graduated in 1894 and became a schoolteacher. Four years later, she married industrialist Joseph G. Wilkins and left teaching to become a housewife and take care of their four children. Tragically, one of the children died after drinking water contaminated with lye.

Throughout her life, Hattie was deeply involved in church activities at Selma's Broad Street Baptist Church.[1] Even though she had a full life with the church and raising her children, Hattie was also deeply involved in politics and social issues, most notably women's rights and, in particular, women's right to vote. With the encouragement of her husband, Hattie became one of the leading suffragists in Alabama and was one of the founders of the Selma Suffrage Association in 1919. She was also a board member of the Alabama Equal Suffrage Association (AESA), which was founded by Pattie Ruffner Jacobs in 1912.

The AESA worked to force passage of the Nineteenth Amendment to the Constitution, granting women the right to vote. The amendment was passed by Congress in June 1919 but was not ratified in Alabama until 1953.

With the amendment now law in much of the country, AESA folded but was reborn as the Alabama League of Women Voters, a chapter of the national organization that helped educate not only women but all Americans about voting and their rights as voters. Hattie Wilkins was one of the founding members of the league.

In 1922, at the age of forty-seven and with the strong wind of the women's movement at her back, Hattie made the decision to run for the Alabama House of Representatives. When her candidacy was announced, newspapers were keen to highlight that she had no political experience; one reported that her "most significant accomplishment [was] that of wife and mother, and maker of a beautiful home."[2] Five women ran for a seat in the statehouse that year, but it was Hattie Hooker Wilkins who won the election, defeating Joseph Green in the general. After her victory over Joseph Green, Hattie said, "When I go to Montgomery, I hope that I may not fail to do at the legislature anything that will be helpful to my state, its women, and its people."[3]

While in office, Hattie presented bills on the House floor to improve education across the state and for health care reform. At the end of her term, Hattie made the decision not to run again, but her time in the House had earned her the respect of her colleagues, who presented her with a beautiful loving cup when she departed inscribed with the words, "To Mrs. Wilkins, the first woman member of the Alabama House of Representatives, a token of esteem from her fellow members, 1923."[4]

Hattie Hooker Wilkins passed away in 1949, but her importance in throwing open the door for women in Alabama politics can not be underestimated. Her career was commemorated in 1977 when she and twenty-five other women were included in a permanent exhibit at the University of Montevallo called *The Faces and Voices of Alabama Women*. She was inducted into the Alabama Women's Hall of Fame in 1997.[5]

---

1. "Hattie Hooker Wilkins (1875–1949)," Alabama Women's Hall of Fame, http://www.awhf.org.
2. Mary Martha Thomas, *Stepping Out of the Shadows: Alabama Women, 1819–1990* (University of Alabama Press, 2021), 155.
3. "Hattie Hooker Wilkins," Alabama Women's Hall of Fame.
4. "Hattie Hooker Wilkins," Alabama Women's Hall of Fame.
5. "Hattie Hooker Wilkins," Encyclopedia of Alabama, https://encyclopediaofalabama.org.

Chapter 49

AUGUSTA EVANS WILSON

The Unreconstructed Rebel

On Christmas Day 1854, fifteen-year-old Augusta Evans presented her father with a very special gift. It was a collection of stories about the Alamo that the young woman heard when her family lived in San Antonio. She titled the manuscript *Inez: A Tale of the Alamo*. Little did she know that this would be the beginning of a highly lucrative writing career that would make Augusta Evans Wilson the first female author to earn over $100,000 despite the many barriers she had to face—most notably being recognized by publishers in the male-dominated literary world. What's even more amazing is that her success came while the country was in the grips of the Civil War.

Augusta was born on May 8, 1835, to Matthew and Sarah Evans. Her father was a successful cotton farmer who had earned enough money to build the family a glorious mansion in Columbus, Georgia, which he called Sherwood. According to people who knew her, Augusta was an exceptionally bright child and had a photographic memory that allowed her to vividly recall sights, sounds and events years after they occurred. Augusta was educated by her mother, Sarah, whom years later she credited for her success. "[She] is in every sense my 'Alma Mater,' the one to whom I owe everything and whom I reverence more than all else on earth."[1]

When Augusta was five, a series of encounters with Native Americans on their farm, a devastating flood in 1841 that the family barely survived and a sudden and rapid decline in the price of cotton wiped the family out financially. With nothing left, they moved to Texas near San Antonio just after the famous Battle of the Alamo between the United States and Mexico

The "Un-Reconstructed Rebel," author Augusta Evans Wilson, was the first woman to earn over $100,000 as an author. *Mobile Public Library Local History & Genealogy.*

was fought. When the family arrived, images of that fierce battle were still fresh in the town's memory, and they left a deep impression on the now ten-year-old Augusta.

Four years later, the Evans family found themselves once again down on their luck and moved again, this time to the Alabama port city of Mobile. Once they were settled into their new home, the images from the stories she had heard in San Antonio about the Alamo kept playing in Augusta's mind. They were so vivid that she felt compelled to put them to paper. She wrote the stories in complete secrecy until Christmas Day 1854, when she presented *Inez: A Tale of the Alamo* to her father. Her father was so impressed with her writing that he presented the manuscript to Augusta's uncle, Augustus Howard, who offered to pay Harper Publishing in New York City to publish the book, to which Harper agreed. On its release, critics panned the book as nothing more than a "bad novel," saying the author had not been exposed to enough literature and that the text was virtually plotless. Augusta was also criticized for espousing a deep anti-Catholic sentiment throughout the book.

The book was not successful, but instead of walking away, Augusta dug in, determined to prove the critics wrong. Following the release of *Inez*, Augusta picked up the Southern cause, and her writing became more political. In 1859, she penned a series of four unsigned letters that appeared in the *Mobile Advertiser*. She did not defend the South or the institution of slavery but instead went on the attack against the North and its literary world—its writers, authors and journalists—saying that the lies Northern publishers and newspapers spewed daily in the name of the almighty dollar were the real immorality in the country. In the first letter, she declared that worrying only about making a buck was "a disgrace to [the] authors and insulting to the intelligence of the American people."[2]

In one letter, she listed her views on the differences between the North and South:

> *The South is genial and idealistic while the North is cold and indifferent; the South is refined while the North only has a love of money that corrupts them; Southern writers write from the heart with beauty while Northern writers are only commercial product; and Southerners cherish their culture and non-partisan values of literature while the North debases literature for political gains.*

Augusta finished writing her second novel by the age of eighteen. Titled *Beulah*, the book tells the story of an orphan who becomes the ward of a wealthy doctor who eventually falls in love with her. The story revolves around the girl's fight with spiritual skepticism, a subject she touched on earlier in *Inez*. The book was rejected by one New York publisher, but undaunted, Augusta resubmitted it, this time taking it in person along with her cousin, John Jones, to Derby and Jackson Publishing in New York City. As the story goes, J.C. Derby took the manuscript and brought it home for his family to read. They were enthralled with the tale and told him to publish it right away. He did, in 1859, and it sold over twenty thousand copies in nine months. With the royalties from the book, Augusta could purchase her family a new home on Mobile's Springhill Avenue that they called the Georgia Cottage.

The letters Augusta penned earlier that year were the beginning of the author's propagandist writings. She went on to attack any Southern author who opposed secession, even breaking ties with a close friend of hers, author Marion Harland, for refusing to leave her Yankee husband and continuing to live "among the oppressors of the only free people left upon the American continent."[3]

Augusta's devotion to the South only intensified. She became friends with many Confederate statesmen and generals. She was honored with a tea party thrown in her honor in the state's capital, Montgomery, while Jefferson Davis was forming his new cabinet. Alabama state legislator Jabez Lamar Monroe Curry is known to have changed a few of his speeches based on suggestions made by Augusta. And when she wrote to

Confederate General Pierre Beauregard about her upcoming novel, he took time out from his duties on the battlefield to write her a full and complete report of the Battles of Bull Run and Manassas, which she would later incorporate into her third book.

Augusta's Southern patriotism was not only political in nature, however. She had deep compassion for the soldiers who were fighting the battles. A camp was set up near her home on Springhill Avenue that would take care of sick and injured soldiers. It was named Camp Beulah in honor of her book. She became a nurse and pitched in to help not only at Camp Beulah but also at Fort Morgan, just south of Mobile on the Alabama Gulf Coast, and Chickamauga, near Atlanta. Augusta would not only tend to the men's wounds but also brighten their spirits by singing to them.

With the Civil War and Southern secession as the backdrop of her life, Augusta began writing her third novel, *Macaria: Altars of Sacrifice*, in 1862. Due to severe shortages of supplies in the South, particularly printing materials, the book was published by West and Johnson in 1863 on brown wrapping paper. The covers were simple boards wrapped in wallpaper. Even so, the book became very popular in both the North and South, and while the subject matter was neither explicitly anti-Union nor anti-North, it was a solid piece of Southern propaganda with a heavy pro-South slant, so much so that the commander of Union forces in Tennessee, General George Henry Thomas, had copies of the book confiscated from his troops and burned.

Augusta had no idea that a publisher in New York, Michael Doolady, had published unauthorized copies of the book. When word reached her first New York publisher and friend, J.C. Derby, that Doolady was trying to capitalize on the book's success with an unauthorized version, Derby decided it was time to pay a visit to the publisher. Derby secretly went to see Doolady and demanded that all royalties from this bootleg version be put into a trust for the author until the end of the war. Derby won the battle, and the publisher agreed. When the war ended, Augusta traveled to New York to visit her old friend Derby in hopes of raising some money to help her brother Howard recover from an injury he had suffered in the war. It was a huge surprise when she learned about the sizeable amount of money that had accumulated from sales of the unauthorized copy of the book.

When the war ended in 1865, it was time to make amends and heal the country, but some wounds are hard to mend. Augusta was invited to attend a special dinner in her honor in New York City. The event was organized by Charles O'Connor, who invited renowned authors and journalists from across the country, one of whom was Henry J. Raymond, the editor of *The*

New York Times. Augusta refused to meet with him because of his "attitude" during the war.

Now a wealthy author, Miss Gusta, as Mobilians called her, set out on a new mission. She began to raise funds to bring the bodies of soldiers who hailed from Mobile and had died in the war back home to their city to rest in peace. A section of Magnolia Cemetery on Virginia Street in Mobile, the second-oldest cemetery in the state's oldest city, was set aside for just that purpose.

In 1868, Augusta married widower and successful grocery store owner Lorenzo Madison Wilson. Prior to her death, Augusta's heart seemed to have softened toward the North—or at least the women of the North. A close friend presented her with a book that was dedicated to the women of both the North and the South. Augusta looked at it and said, "Ah, well. The women of the North as well as of the South are good and true." Her heart may have softened a bit, but she remained what many have called her, an "unreconstructed rebel," unable to reconcile the results of the war.

In all, Augusta wrote nine novels before her death in 1909, including her most popular, *St. Elmo* (1866), which sold over forty million copies in four months. The author's funeral was quite the occasion in the Port City. Newspaper accounts reported that a procession of thirty carriages carried her body to Magnolia Cemetery. Lines of cars filled with people followed the procession, and several hundred Mobilians were waiting graveside for the entourage to arrive. When the final prayers were read and Augusta laid to rest, those in attendance refused to leave, and the gates of the cemetery had to remain open long past closing time.[4] It was a fitting tribute to the woman who broke a barrier for female writers around the world, a woman dedicated to her cause, the "Unreconstructed Rebel"—Miss Gusta.

---

1. Joe Cuhaj, *Hidden History of Mobile* (The History Press, 2019), 70.
2. Mrs. Johnson, "Augusta Evans Wilson: A Paper Given by Mrs. Johnson at the October 1956 Meeting of the New Idea Study Club," Mobile Public Library Local History and Genealogy, October 1959.
3. William Perry Fidler, "Augusta Evans Wilson as Confederate Propagandist," *Alabama Review* (January 1949), 42.
4. "Augusta Evans Wilson Buried in Magnolia," *Mobile Register*, May 11, 1909.

Chapter 50

TAMMY WYNETTE

The First Lady of Country Music

From hard hours working as a youngster on the family cotton farm to country and pop music stardom, Tammy Wynette paid her dues and then some, and throughout her life and storied music career, she overcame many of life's obstacles to become the First Lady of Country Music.

The story begins in Itawamba, Mississippi, in 1942 with the birth of Virginia Wynette Pugh, later to be renamed for her singing career—Tammy. Her father, William Hollice, died when she was less than a year old due to a brain tumor. William loved music and left his young daughter a recording of himself singing and playing guitar with the hope that one day his daughter would latch onto music in her life.[1]

After Virginia's father's passing, her mother, Mildred, remarried and left her daughter to be raised by her grandparents on a family farm in Red Bay, Alabama. The family struggled to make ends meet, and by the age of seven, Virginia was helping the family tend to the fields, including endless hours of picking cotton. Virginia would never forget those meager days on the farm, and until her death, she always kept a bowl with cotton balls in it to remind her.[2]

When Viriginia was seventeen, she married the first of her five husbands, Euple Byrd. Because she was underage, her grandfather had to sign the marriage papers. Euple was an itinerant construction worker, which meant the couple was constantly moving as he tried to find work. According to Virginia's biography, Euple was unemployed more often than not.[3] The couple ended up moving into an abandoned house with no plumbing. They also had two daughters together, Gwen and Jaclyn.

Virginia finally became tired of living penniless, and with a little financial help from her family, she attended beauty school in Tupelo, Mississippi. From that moment on, even during the height of her music career, Virginia made sure her beautician license was kept up to date, just in case.

The couple moved to Birmingham, where they had their third child, a daughter, who was premature, weighing in at one pound, eight ounces at birth. At four months old, the child nearly died from spinal meningitis. Eventually, Virginia's marriage to Euple fell apart, and the couple divorced in 1965, forcing her to pull double duty to raise three young children. Not only did she work ten hours a day as a beautician, but she also landed a job singing on a local Birmingham television show, *The Country Boy Eddie Show*. So after a long day in the beauty shop, she would have to wake up at four o'clock the next morning to appear on the show.

That same year, Virginia regularly traveled the nearly two hundred miles from Birmingham to Nashville to audition with recording companies in hopes of landing a contract, but she was rejected time and time again. She finally made the decision to move herself and her children to Nashville full time. It was a gamble, to say the least—moving to a new city with no job, no place to live and three children in tow—but it was one that paid off.

In December 1965, she auditioned with one of the most influential country music producers and songwriters of the day, Billy Sherrill. Sherrill was signing artists to Epic Records at the time, and when he heard Virginia sing, he was sold, but he thought her name was not very memorable. According to music historians, Sherrill thought Virginia bore a striking resemblance to actress Debbie Reynolds in her starring role in the movie *Tammy*. "You look like a Tammy to me," he told her, and Tammy Wynette was born.[4]

The first song Tammy recorded for Epic was written by country singer Johnny Paycheck, "Apartment #9." The song rose to No. 44 on the country music charts in December 1966, but that was only a hint of what was to come. Over the next four years, Tammy's next eleven albums went straight to No. 1, winning her two Grammy Awards and three Country Music Association Female Artist of the Year awards.

Tammy's biggest-selling single was a song written by her producer, Billy Sherrill, "Stand By Your Man." The song was released in 1968 and hit No. 1 on the country charts, where it stayed for three straight weeks. It also went to No. 19 on the pop music charts and No. 1 in Europe. In all, it sold over two million copies, and it was added to the Library of Congress's National Recording Registry.

Over the years, "Stand By Your Man" has been interpreted in many ways. As the Library of Congress points out, the song's opening lyric, "Sometimes it's hard to be a woman," resonated with many female listeners in the 1960s. But the song was also interpreted as saying, "If your man is unfaithful, stick with him" because of lines like "But if you love him, you'll forgive him"—at which Tammy took umbrage.

> *I don't see anything in that song that implies a woman is supposed to sit home and raise babies while a man goes out and raises hell.... To me it means: be supportive of your man; show him you love him and you're proud of him; and be willing to forgive him if he doesn't always live up to your image of what he should be.*[5]

The song's message would be put to the test in Tammy's real life when she married her third husband, country star George Jones. The couple married in 1969, a union of two country music superstars that captivated fans around the world. They recorded numerous songs together and had one daughter, Georgette, but Jones's well-known battle with alcoholism was the downfall of the fairytale marriage, and they divorced in 1975.

Tammy married again, in 1976, to Michael Tomlin, a marriage that was annulled after only forty-four days. She went on to marry her final husband, her longtime friend and songwriter George Richey, in 1978. In her book *The Three of Us: Growing Up with George & Tammy*, her daughter Georgette wrote that Richey was an abusive husband.[6] Nevertheless, the couple stayed married until her death.

In the 1990s, Tammy Wynette's health began to deteriorate. She was in severe pain and became increasingly dependent on pain medication. She passed away at home in her sleep on April 6, 1998, at the young age of fifty-five. Three days after her death, country music fans and celebrities gathered at the Ryman Auditorium, the home of the Grand Ole Opry (also known as the Mother Church of Country Music)—of which Tammy became a member in 1969—to pay tribute to the First Lady of Country Music on a worldwide television broadcast.

In the end, Tammy Wynette sold over thirty million records in her career, grossing over $1 million. She scored twenty No. 1 hits and was the first female country singer to sell over one million albums. Just months after her death, Tammy was inducted into the Country Music Hall of Fame with words that summed up her life and career nicely: "Her 'steel magnolia' image allowed her to work within a male-dominated environment in which prejudices against women were still strong. If she has been the victim, she has also been the survivor."[7]

---

1. Mary A. Bufwack, "Tammy Wynette," Country Music Hall of Fame, https://www.countrymusichalloffame.org.
2. "Tammy Wynette Bio," TammyWynette.com, March 9, 2017, https://tammywynette.com.
3. "Tammy Wynette Bio," TammyWynette.com.
4. Chuck Dauphin, "Billy Sherrill, Country Producer Behind George Jones, Tammy Wynette, & More, Dies at 78," *Billboard Magazine*, August 4, 2015, https://www.billboard.com.
5. Cary O'Dell, "'Stand by Your Man'—Tammy Wynette (1968)," Library of Congress, https://www.loc.gov.
6. Samantha Drake, "The Story Behind Tammy Wynette's Tragic Life," *Country Living Magazine*, November 29, 2022, https://www.countryliving.com.
7. Bufwack, "Tammy Wynette."

ABOUT THE AUTHOR

Joe Cuhaj grew up in northern New Jersey, where his love of history was nurtured by his history-loving family and exceptional high school history teachers. The former radio broadcaster moved to Mobile, Alabama, with his wife, who is from the Port City, over forty years ago and immediately fell in love with the city's rich history and culture that dates back over 320 years. It was a love that inspired him to write three nonfiction history titles about the city for Arcadia Publishing/The History Press: *Baseball in Mobile*, *Hidden History of Mobile* and *A History Lover's Guide to Mobile and the Alabama Gulf Coast*. Joe has written a total of twenty books: outdoor recreation titles, short stories and other nonfiction history books. You can learn more about his books and upcoming releases on his website, http://www.joe-cuhaj.com.